THE SUPREME COURT:
politicians in robes

Charles H. Sheldon
Southampton College
Southampton, New York

GLENCOE PRESS
A Division of The Macmillan Company
Beverly Hills
Collier-Macmillan Ltd., London

GLENCOE PRESS
A Division of The Macmillan Company
8701 Wilshire Boulevard
Beverly Hills, California 90211
Collier-Macmillan Canada, Ltd., Toronto, Canada

Library of Congress catalog card number: 71-104867

First printing, 1970

Contents

3. Church and State: The Role of Religion in the American Constitutional System   63

4. Democratic Representation: One Man — One Vote   88

5. Freedom of Expression: Pornography and the Law   112

Supplementary Reading List   137

The Insight Series

Studies in Contemporary Issues

from Glencoe Press

Series Editors: Fred Krinsky and Joseph Boskin

Preface

In our efforts to understand the American political system we are often forced to study the many diverse and complicated political institutions in isolation. We examine, for example, Congress, the Presidency or the Supreme Court as separate institutions with their own unique functions within the American political context, but we frequently forget that institutions are closely interrelated. Politics is a complicated phenomenon involving a myriad of interdependent forces. The nine Justices of the Supreme Court, like Congress and the President, are involved in all the major issues that face American society today. By following the actions of the Court, the reactions to its decisions and the subsequent responses on the part of the Justices themselves, a clearer understanding of the web of government that is the American political system is possible. It is this interaction which is the subject of this collection.

Obviously a book attempting to illustrate the web of government can only present the highlights. Thus, the materials herein presented are only gross examples of American politics in which the Court plays a leading role. The student must go beyond these materials to grasp the subleties of American government and politics. Such a search can be tremendously rewarding. This collection must be regarded as only a beginning.

The author wishes to thank many people for the encouragement and assistance they gave in collecting, analyzing and preparing the materials included in this book. Dr. James R. Klonoski should receive a belated thanks for turning the author on. Dr. Donald G. Baker has helped sustain this interest. I am further indebted to Mrs. Harriet Vail, Mrs. Pat Winters, Miss Martha Mollik and Mr. James Murdock for their assistance in typing and preparing the manuscript. Acknowledgement must also be given the political science students at Southampton College who, through their desire to know, inspired this collection.

C.H.S.

Southampton, New York
July, 1969

Introduction

The appointment of Earl Warren as Chief Justice of the United States in 1953 marked the opening of a new period in our Constitutional development. In the next fifteen years the Supreme Court rewrote, with profound social consequence, major constitutional doctrines governing race relations, the administration of criminal justice, and the operation of the political process. The extent and rapidity of the changes raise grave questions concerning the proper role of the Supreme Court in our national development—questions concerning the nature and function of constitutional adjudication.

> Archibald Cox, *The Warren Court:*
> *Constitutional Decision as an*
> *Instrument of Reform (1968)*

Not since the late thirties has the American public been as aware of the crucial role of the Supreme Court in the American political system as in the 1960s. The Warren Court has symbolized "judicial activism." The impact of the Court has been felt in many diverse areas of American life. The condition of the blacks in white America was initially pointed out to most Americans by the Supreme Court. The rights of the accused at the stationhouse and courthouse were projected into the political arena by the high court. The role of religion in American public life and the meaning of representation in federal, state, and local legislative bodies were given a new course by the Justices. Attempts to define the limits of artistic freedom also brought the Court into public controversy. If not revolutionary, certainly the changes wrought by the highest court in these areas must be regarded as bold innovations coming from what has been regarded as a passive branch of the government.

At the very least, the Supreme Court has awakened the American public to the broad implications of the Bill of Rights and the Fourteenth Amendment. People, groups and governments have reacted, sometimes vehemently. These reactions illustrate the political nature of the judicial process, for the Court's decision is often the beginning—not the end— of the controversy. The subject of this book is exactly this relationship between Supreme Court decisions, the reactions of major elements within the American system, and the reactions of the Court itself in subsequent rulings.

Five subject areas have been chosen to illustrate the impact of Supreme Court decisions on the political system generally. These are (1) the development of the rights of Negroes, beginning with the desegregation case of 1954 (*Brown* v. *Board of Education*); (2) the growth of the rights of the accused in criminal cases, beginning with right to counsel (*Gideon* v. *Wainwright*); (3) the meaning of the religion clauses of the First Amendment involving prayers in the classroom (*Engel* v. *Vitale*); (4) representation in legislative bodies, or the "one man, one vote" principle of reapportionment (*Baker* v. *Carr*); and (5) obscenity and the law (*Roth* v. *U.S.*).

None of these issues was settled by the Supreme Court. Quite the contrary, these were not political issues for most Americans until the Supreme Court acted. Thus, the Supreme Court has been at the beginning of the political process rather than at the end. Furthermore, the Court does not rule and then withdraw into "splendid isolation." Each of these major issues has involved further litigation. For example, the Court's ruling in *Brown* v. *Board of Education* reversed the long established principle of "separate but equal." The Court, in 1954, declared separate facilities to be "inherently unequal" and therefore in conflict with the "equal protection" clause of the Fourteenth Amendment. Although originally limited to public education, subsequent legislative and judicial action has applied the *Brown* doctrine to all aspects of public accommodations. These changes have not been unopposed and principally resort to the traditional control of public education by state and local governments.

Gideon v. *Wainwright* granted to the accused in the state courts the right to have a lawyer at the trial stage without consideration of ability to pay. Soon the Court's supervision of procedure led to a recognition of the right to counsel at the very beginning of the investigatory stages of police activity and to strict protections against coerced confessions. Thus, the Fifth and Sixth Amendments of the Bill of Rights have been extended to state as well as federal judicial proceedings. But many people argue that the protection of the accused has been enhanced at the cost of hampering the ability of the police to fight crime.

Yet another controversy stems from that part of the First Amendment which reads, "Congress shall make no law respecting an establishment of religion, or prohibiting the free exercise thereof; . . . " This has come to mean that governments, at any level, should not be involved in religious activities. In two cases, the Supreme Court declared official prayers and bible readings in public schools to be unconstitutional as a form of establishment (*Engel* v. *Vitale* and *Abington School District* v.

Schempp). A substantial number of Americans, however, viewed this judicial "intervention" as a restriction of their right to "free exercise of religion."

To what degree should the Supreme Court interfere with the "political" branches of the governmental system? The Court's answer came in a series of reapportionment cases, beginning in 1962 with *Baker v. Carr*. Issues dealing with the composition of representative bodies could now become a concern of the courts when unproportional representation of legislative bodies deprived people of the "equal protection of the laws." Had the Court thus usurped the prerogatives of both the state legislatures and the citizens themselves? To many the answer was a clear "yes."

In *Roth v. U.S.* the Supreme Court created a fifth controversy by attempting to define the limits of artistic candor. The test of obscenity was "whether to the average person, applying contemporary community standards, the dominant theme of the material taken as a whole appeals to prurient interests." Obscene material, thus defined, was not accorded the protection of the First Amendment which is given to other printed or spoken matter. On the other hand, the Court also ruled that "all ideas having even the slightest redeeming social importance" would fall within the First Amendment guarantees of freedom of speech and of the press. The "social value" doctrine has become the test (*Memoirs v. Massachusetts*), thereby involving the Supreme Court in a political controversy quite as intense as those in which the Court has been embroiled in other areas.

The Supreme Court's decisions in these five constitutional areas have involved the Justices in the politics of the American system. The jurists of the high court are not protected from politics merely because they wear the robes symbolic of judicial independence and objectivity. They are politicians in robes.

But the Court is doing more than merely deciding cases with political ramifications. The Justices of the Supreme Court are raising issues which go to the very essence of our democracy. Questions about equality, rule of law, religion and the state, democratic representation and morality have been posed directly to the American people, and the people have responded with a diversity of answers. The Supreme Court has asked America what it is all about, and America has been compelled to seek answers. Some of the responses have been attacks on the source of the questions, but others have called for re-evaluation of the way America sees itself.

The responses to the Court's decisions are expressed through Congress, the Presidency, state political institutions, pressure groups and public opinion. In each case, the nature of the response is different. Congress has proposed constitutional amendments to change Court decisions and passed laws to correct or extend constitutional interpretations. It has subjected Court appointees to painful interrogation and probed into the affairs of Justices already on the Court. In addition, it has been the major forum in which the issues raised by the Court have been debated.

The President, who has primary responsibility for enforcing high court rulings, may react enthusiastically or reluctantly. His public pronouncements influence greatly public compliance with new constitutional directions. Although Congress shares the responsibility, it is the President who has the initiative in naming new members for the Supreme Court. The Chief Executive must also respond indirectly to Court decisions by his actions regarding proposed legislation. The patterns of his responses are as myriad as that of Congress.

States, who recently have felt the brunt of high court decisions, have reacted in a variety of ways. New legislation, manifestos, delaying tactics, pressures on the federal government and electoral office campaigns are all responses to the issues generated by the Supreme Court.

Finally, the public reacts through compliance or noncompliance. The degree of popular support is expressed through opinion polls, political party activities and pressure group tactics. These efforts, in turn, find outlets at the state and national levels. Clearly, each innovative decision or series of decisions by the Supreme Court creates a web of forces involving virtually all of the major political institutions comprising the American political system.

But the Justices too are part of the continuing debate. All the major issues herein discussed involved a series of cases. The Court thus can rejoin the political dialogue. In *Baker* v. *Carr*, the Court opened the door to changes in representation at the national, state and local levels. Seven years later the Court, in *Wells* v. *Rockefeller*, was still acting on its own ruling when it declared New York State's Congressional districting plan inconsistent with the doctrine of "one man, one vote." The Supreme Court remains in the political arena.

It is the purpose of this book of readings to document the impact of the Supreme Court on the political system of America. These five "trouble areas" have not been chosen merely because they are controversial, but because they represent the substantial changes wrought in the American system by the Supreme Court in the last two decades. The book will attempt to illustrate the political role of the highest court in the American system. The Justices, although they might choose to deny it, are politicians. Often a Court decision represents the end of an issue, but in many cases it serves to project an issue directly into the center of political debate. The following pages illustrate the drama of this process.

The Political Power of the Court (1969)*

The Supreme Court is a unique American institution. No other major nation assigns to its highest court the broad power to overrule the decisions of its executives and its national legislature if it deems those decisions unconstitutional.

Because of the power of judicial review, the Supreme Court is never very far from the heart of political controversy. As Justice Robert H. Jackson once observed, "Most questions which have deeply agitated our people [have] found their way to the Supreme Court in the guise of private controversies between litigating parties."

Since society divides on great issues, it is natural that the Supreme Court, which is often the final arbiter of those issues, recurrently experiences external attack and internal division. Equally recurrent is the wishful belief that controversy could be stilled if only the Court had a Chief Justice who could harmonize the views of its members, or if the justice had more prior judicial experience and less intimate acquaintance with government and elective politics, or if the justices would simply read the Constitution as it was written and not try to interpret it in the light of their own social philosophies.

President Nixon in his news conference last week touched on all of these myths in discussing the background of his selection of Judge Warren E. Burger to be Chief Justice. The President said he had particularly sought "a leadership quality" in his prospective nominee. But it is highly doubtful that any Chief Justice can reconcile the views of strong-minded colleagues either by personal charm or forceful advocacy in the weekly conference.

. . . .

Thirty years ago liberals were incensed that a conservative Supreme Court should overrule economic reform legislation. Today conservatives are incensed that a liberal Supreme Court should overrule state courts on issues of criminal procedure. Now as in the past, these controversies in the law reflect controversies in the larger society.

Problems in criminal law, for example, are not separable from changing attitudes toward race and the rights of the poor.

In choosing Judge Burger, a conservative with a strong law-and-order image, President Nixon has made a political choice. It is political, not in the sense of party affiliation or Senatorial clearances—Mr. Nixon was slaying strawmen in disavowing that kind of politics—but in the broader sense that the Court's own function is political.

The President deliberately chose a man who would act upon the more conservative philosophy which Mr. Nixon favors. The power to make that choice is one of the most coveted prerogatives of a President, and there is no reason why Mr. Nixon should not exercise it. The Court is now likely to move significantly in a more conservative direction, particularly if, as is probable, President Nixon soon appoints another judge of similar viewpoint. Presidents usually try to shape the judicial future, and Mr. Nixon has begun his own effort to do so. Only time and opportunity can determine his success.

The Warren Era: A Conversation with Former Chief Justice Earl Warren (1969)*

In the following interview published immediately following his retirement, Earl Warren summarizes his view of the issues, legal and political, surrounding the Supreme Court during his 16 years as Chief Justice.

Q. Mr. Chief Justice, you have devoted more than 50 years to the law as a young legislative clerk, as District Attorney, as Governor, as Attorney General, and as Chief Justice of the United States. In what significant ways would you say the administration has changed over the past half century?

A. Of course, the principles of the administration of justice have changed very little. We have the same constitution, generally speaking, the same substantive law, but of course the size of our population, the number of crimes committed, the number of judges who administer the law, and all of the personnel that is essential to do that have

---

*Reprinted with permission from McClatchy Broadcasting, Sacramento, California. Mr. Morrie Landsberg, editor, McClatchy Broadcasting interviewed Earl Warren in connection with his retirement, on June 23, 1969, as the 14th Chief Justice of the United States.

greatly changed the manner of administering the law and that change has brought with it a great many problems that didn't exist. Judges formerly had a rather leisurely life, but these days they are pressed for time in everything they do, and pressed as much as they may be, there is always a backlog that distresses a judge and retards the administration of justice. This is one of the common problems that we must face in the near future.

. . . .

Q. Way back in 1925, in your days as a prosecutor, you were quoted as saying, "If people have money, they are likely to escape punishment." To what extent would you say our justice is class conscious today?

A. Well, that is a rather abstract statement, but just the same there is a lot to it. The person without the means of investigating his case without having a skilled lawyer is at a disadvantage that a person of means would not be at, and naturally that is reflected in the number of people who are convicted and many times from the punishment that they receive.

Q. But have there been changes since 1925 which have made legal counsel more available to the poor?

A. Oh yes! Since I have been on this court, the court has determined that everyone is entitled to a lawyer. If he cannot afford it himself, the state or the nation, whichever it may be, must furnish counsel for him. But the problem is to get counsel who will work on the cases and do the things that are necessary to see that a man's rights, whatever they may be, are fully protected.

Q. Mr. Chief Justice, in recent years critics have contended the Supreme Court decisions coddle the criminal and encourage crime. What do you say to this from your perspective?

A. I am of the opinion that the decisions of the courts, and I am speaking now of this court in particular which has established the guidelines for the courtroom, have in no way adversely affected the prosecution of crime. Certainly, every man is entitled to a lawyer. No man, whether he is rich or poor, whether he is educated or uneducated, is qualified to go into a courtroom knowing nothing of the law or its procedures, is qualified to defend himself in a time of crisis such as that. He is entitled to someone who can look at his case objectively, study it, and study what his rights might be and then present it to the court. I think great advances have been made in recent years, but still there are many parts of the country where even the assignment of counsel is not done with any great degree of seriousness.

Perhaps they will appoint someone to represent a man in the next half hour and they will go through a trial in a day and it will be all over. That is not representation and thoughtful lawyers and the bar association and defendants' association are working very diligently on that now to see that every man gets the proper representation of his rights, whatever they might be. A man might be guilty and confess his guilt and admit his guilt, but still he has certain rights in the courtroom that ought to be presented to the court in determining what the punishment should be.

Q. There are people who feel the court's critics overlook the fact that the rights of individuals—all individuals—are involved in these decisions. Do you agree?

A. Oh yes! There are so many people who believe that, for instance, any decision that might help a man who is charged with being a communist is coddling communists. Of course, that is not true, but a man, whether he is a communist, or a fascist, or a klu klux klanner, or whatever it might be, is entitled to have his rights protected in the courtroom and if his rights cannot be protected in the courtroom, the rights of no one can be secure.

· ·

Q. Recalling your experiences as District Attorney of Alameda County and Attorney General of California, would you say the court's decisions have made police work more difficult?

A. I suppose one can honestly say that if you follow rules in any business, your work is more difficult than if you just are left to your own devices, some of them even brutal devices, but not more difficult in the sense that they should not be performed. But if, instead of beating a prisoner to get a confession from him, he is given a lawyer and given an opportunity to talk to him and then the police are enabled to talk to him after that . . . is a rule that . . . it is just so much a question of common humanity that nobody should want to avoid it.

· ·

Q. Mr. Chief Justice, the late Justice Felix Frankfurter said in 1946, if I may quote, "It is hostile to a democratic system to involve the judiciary in the politics of the people." Have you ever felt that the Supreme Court's jurisdiction should be limited?

A. Well, it is very much limited and always has been and, of course, judges when they take the bench are supposed to detach themselves from politics, I don't mean become disinterested because every American citizen should be interested in politics, but a judge should detach himself from active politics and it has been my experience that most judges with whom I have ever come in contact have obeyed that rule.

Q. Did you feel in the early phase that the court was going it alone in protecting civil rights and liberties?

A. Well, there was a long time, from the 1870's until 15 years or so ago, that Congress passed no laws affecting the civil liberties of the people. That was not entirely the fault of the Congress because the court itself had, in those early years, put some limitations upon the acts of Congress. But because there were no laws passed during that time and because problems involving civil rights were developing, the only refuge people had was in the courts, and the only law that the court could apply was the broad principles of the Constitution and that made a very, very difficult situation for the courts and we were very much alone at that time. But since that time, Congress has passed a number of civil rights laws which encompass a great many of the civil rights and I am sure that will mean the work of the courts will be easier now than it has been in the past.

Q. Were you at times impatient that state and federal officials were not responsive enough in the desegregation matter?

A. In some parts of the country, yes. One couldn't help being impatient when he would see the orders of the court flaunted and just not obeyed in any sense of the word, and where illegal things were changed in form, but not in substance and carried on. Of course, one feels frustrated at that, but there are so many things that have happened to encourage one who has been in this field that I think on the whole, much progress has been made.

Q. I know the court doesn't try to run a popularity poll, but do you feel there has been a general acceptance by the public of recent decisions on such matters as desegregation and civil liberties?

A. That is very difficult for me to say, but I think in the main, the people of this country recognize that the great American ideal is that everyone shall be entitled to equal protection under the laws and while they might disagree with the application of it in something that irritates them particularly, still they have the consciousness that it is not only the law, but that it is right. I think in that sense the American people are in favor of the overall objectives of the Fourteenth Amendment of the Constitution of the United States which guarantees those rights.

·   ·   ·   ·   ·   ·   ·   ·   ·   ·   ·   ·   ·   ·   ·   ·   ·   ·

Q. Would you say, Mr. Chief Justice, that American justice has been completely desegregated?

A. Oh no, by no means! There aren't 20% of the school children in the south that are in desegregated schools. The same situation exists in some of our northern cities. The black people do not have work opportunities that white people have. They're still having problems in voting in some parts of the country, and no we just haven't put all of our force behind giving people equal rights and that, to me, would be the answer to many of our problems. When the American people, as a whole, recognize that we have, in the past, been wrong in depriving certain minorities of their constitutional rights and when we make the decision to see that they will, in the future, have these rights, then I think we're on the way to solving most of our domestic problems.

Q. What would you list, Mr. Chief Justice, as the Supreme Court's most important decision in your 16 years here? Was it the school desegregation or reapportionment?

A. I think the reapportionment, not only of State legislatures, but of representative government in this country is perhaps the most important issue we have had before the Supreme Court. If everyone in this country has an opportunity to participate in his government on equal terms with everyone else, and can share in electing representatives who will be truly representative of the entire community and not some special interest, then most of these problems that we are now confronted with would be solved through the political process rather than through the courts.

Q. Would this apply mostly to the South?

A. I remember the first case we had, the Baker vs. Carr case, came from one of our northern states and that the legislature in that state had been the same for over 60 years in spite of all the territorial changes. The group that was in power kept the legislature apportioned just exactly as it was over 60 years before, although the State Constitution said that the representation should be equal, but they paid no attention to it. The courts, prior to Baker vs. Carr, said that it was the business of legislatures and not of courts. This court held that the question of whether a person was having equal protection of the laws was a judicial question and we had the right to decide it and we held that the legislatures must give equal representation to everyone. That was where the expression "one man one vote" came into being and, of course, it just isn't state legislatures, but it has been expanded to the Congress and expanded also to local government. If it's right on one level of government, of course, it's right on all levels of government, and in that sense, I think, the case which all the other reapportionment cases followed is perhaps the most important case that we have had since I have been on the court.

Q. In another area, you said awhile back that pornography was the court's most difficult area. Why is that?

A. It's the most difficult area for the simple reason that we have to balance two constitutional rights with each other. Of course, the state and national government have a right to have a decent society and have the right to make the laws and regulations that will keep it a decent society. On the other hand, we have the First Amendment which says Congress shall pass no laws abridging the right of speech and the press and religion, and so forth, and the question is how far people go under the First Amendment which gives them freedom of speech without offending the right of the government to maintain a decent society, and when you have those two things coming together, you find it very difficult to write a verbal definition of what obscenity is. I know that in many communities in the past, they have had boards of censorship and the experience that was had under them was atrocious. I recall that in one southern city, the censorship board—board of censorship—ruled that a motion picture which showed little colored children and little white children playing in a school yard was obscene. I remember, also, another instance when in Chicago the police board of censorship, in spite of all that goes on in that great city, held that Walt Disney's picture of a vanishing prairie which showed a mother buffalo giving birth to her little one in a snow storm was obscene. Many other instances of things of that kind show how far boards of censorship will go in determining what is obscene and what is not obscene. When it comes to writing a definition, it is very difficult to do it. The court has done its best, but the people on both sides of the question will stretch it just as far as they can and make tremendous problems.

. . . .

Q. Is it up to the postal authorities or is it a weakness in the law?

A. Well, I don't like to point the finger at anybody, but it is a question of law enforcement and those who say that the Supreme Court has put its approval on obscenity are just not aware of the facts because the court has not done that. The court has specifically said that obscenity is not protected under the free speech clause of the constitution. The only question involved is what is obscenity, and I haven't seen anyone who has been able to write the definition for obscenity that juries can follow that has been fairly satisfactory.

. . . .

Q. Mr. Chief Justice, do you believe the Bill of Rights would be ratified if it came to a vote today?

A. I think probably that there would be a great debate over some of them because we have never taught our youngsters in the schools, or today are we teaching them in most of our colleges where the Bill of Rights came from, why it is there, and what its purpose is in society. There are a lot of thoughtless people who feel that we don't need any more Fifth Amendment, we don't need any more jury trials under the Sixth Amendment, and we don't need protection as to free speech and freedom of the press and freedom of religion, but I do believe that on sober second thought after a great debate, the American people are wise enough to retain those rights which have made this country the greatest in the world.

. . . .

Q. Mr. Chief Justice, what are some of the forces which challenge a free society today?

A. I think that perhaps the most important force is the force of apathy. When the people are not interested in their government, when they're not willing to participate in it and do the things for the general welfare that our institutions complicate, we are really in danger then. And that, I think, stems from the fact that so many people are unaware of the historical background of our institutions, how they came into being, why they came into being, and so forth. I have no fear at all of our future as long as people are interested in government. No matter how they disagree, as long as they are interested in government and will have the great debate in order to get things established, I have no concern about the future at all. American People in the aggregate are wise and they're good and they will decide things in the right way if we can get everybody interested in the affairs of government.

. . . .

Q. What do you say, Mr. Chief Justice, to critics who say that the court, by its decisions, has dealt a death blow to states' rights?

A. Oh, on the contrary, I think that the Supreme Court has established states' rights. What does reapportionment do, but establish states' rights? It establishes in the states the power to govern themselves and most of the problems that we have today in our big cities, for instance, we find they are there because the states have done nothing about them. . . . Once the Federal government does it for them, of course, it has to build up a big bureaucracy in order to administer these programs; so, I think in all respects, I can't think of anything that this court has done to destroy states' rights.

. . . .

Q. Mr. Chief Justice, what was your reaction to the clamor by your critics for your impeachment?

A. Oh, they have a right to do that. I believe that criticism is a proper function in government. No one should be above criticism and while one would rather be praised, I guess, than blamed, I have never had any ill feelings for anyone who criticized the court or even who suggested my impeachment. Although, they knew that there were no grounds for it and it wasn't possible, but they have a right to do it and I have never had any feelings against it.

. . . .

Q. The statement has been made that the court, under your leadership, made laws instead of interpreting the Constitution. What do you say to that?

A. Well, I think that no one could honestly say that the court makes no law. It doesn't make it consciously, it doesn't do it by intending to usurp the role of Congress, but because of the very nature of our job, when Congress says that everyone is entitled to the equal protection of the laws and it enacts no legislation on a given subject, and we have a case in this court in that area, we are left to interpreting the constitutional section one way or the other. We make law. It couldn't be otherwise, but we don't do it for the purpose of usurping Congress' function because Congress can do as it did in the last few years in the Civil Rights area, pass some very important civil rights acts and those acts have made our work immeasurably easier because all we have to do now is say what did Congress mean when it said this, and it said that, and it said something else. Before Congress had said nothing and we had to decide whether it came within that broad language of the Constitution, that everyone is entitled to due process of law and to the equal protection of the laws. Now, normally when we interpret congressional statute, if we misinterpret it, it is of no great significance because Congress within a few days can enact a new law to state exactly what they do mean, but when you come to dealing with constitutional questions, then, of course, it's different. Congress can't overrule our opinions on the Constitution. But sure, we have to make law. When two litigants come into court, one says the Act of Congress means this, the other one says the Act of Congress means the opposite of that, and we say the Act of Congress means something—either one of the two or something in between. We are making law, aren't we? Not because we want to invoke our power as against the Congress, but we have to interpret it and whatever way we interpret it we are making some law. But to recognize that as to statutes, if Congress doesn't believe that we interpreted their law properly they can change it overnight if they wish to do it.

Q. Someone once said, Mr. Chief Justice, that the Warren court, as he put it, will rank in history as the court of the people. Is that the way you'd like the court to be remembered?

A. I would like the court throughout its history to be remembered as the court of the people. No one can say how the opinions of any particular court or any particular era will stand the test of time. All one can do is to do his best to make his opinions conform to the Constitution and laws of the United States and then hope that they'll both be so considered in the future.

Chapter One

America in Black and White:
The Second Emancipation
Proclamation, 1954

May 17, 1954, must be regarded as a fateful day in the history of the Supreme Court as well as a crucial day in the often painful drive for equality for millions in America. After years of litigation the Supreme Court unanimously announced the end of the "separate but equal" doctrine. The decision in *Brown* v. *Board of Education of Topeka** annulled a doctrine which for almost sixty years had permitted the legal separation of blacks and whites.

The Fourteenth Amendment to the United States Constitution demands that

> No state shall . . . deprive any person of life, liberty, or property, without due process of law; nor deny to any person within it jurisdiction the equal protection of the laws.

To the nine Justices of the Supreme Court, this clause applied to any situation in which the laws of a state operated to the detriment of any arbitrarily defined group. The Court established its precedent by ruling that "separate, but equal" was an impossibility, that separation itself created inequality.

> To separate (children) from others of similar age and qualifications solely because of their race generates a feeling of inferiority as to

---

*347 U.S. 483 (1954).

their status in the community that may affect their hearts and minds in a way unlikely to be undone.

Psychological and sociological testimony provided the basis for the Court's decision. The door was thus opened for a revolution in law and in society generally. Discriminatory practices in housing, public accommodations, recreation, and marriage laws all were subject to attack by the new doctrine. The political furor surrounding the Court has had few counterparts in contemporary America.

The *Brown* decision specifically and the politics generated by the ruling were characterized by several unique factors. First, the Supreme Court had been forced to apply the principles of the Declaration of Independence and the Constitution simply because no other political institutions would act. Congress, because key positions were assigned on the basis of seniority, was dominated by Southern conservatives. The President was hampered by party loyalties, Congressional hostility and public opinion. Southern state legislatures and executives were products of—and participants in—a system of white dominance. If action was to be taken, it had to be initiated by litigation brought before the courts. Second, the Justices acknowledged the revolutionary nature of their decision by delaying compliance. A year later the Court, after hearing arguments on methods of implementing the decision, adopted the "with all deliberate speed" formula. The formula would be applied by the lower courts because of their "proximity to local conditions and the possible need for further hearings . . ."† Finally, the 1954 decision was unique in that its greatest impact was felt by a region of the United States whose traditions had relied upon keeping the black population legally, socially and politically separate—the South.

Because of these characteristics the political responses took a fairly predictable form. Congress reacted initially through denunciations, proposed amendments to the Constitution and delaying tactics. The control of committee chairmanships by Southerners prevented Congress from enacting civil rights legislation until 1957. Not until the 1964 Civil Rights Act, ten years after the *Brown* decision, did Congress incorporate the principles of *Brown* into federal legislation.

The states interpreted "all deliberate speed" with the emphasis on "deliberate." In many school districts in the South, classrooms are as segregated today as they were in 1954, and in very few has complete desegregation taken place.

---

†*Brown* v. *Board of Education*, 349 U.S. 294 (1955).

Even though the *Brown* decision had its greatest impact in the South, it also gave the impetus to attacks on schools which were segregated because of living patterns, rather than by law. De facto segregation is characteristic of many Northern urban areas. It remains an unresolved issue.

The course of the social and political struggle which the Court initiated in 1954 has taken many diverse and often contradictory directions. Initially, the goals of the black organizations centered around legal equality, and the methods reflected the concern for legal form. The N.A.A.C.P., largely responsible for the successes in the courts, led the attack. By 1960, the focus had changed to social inequality; many blacks felt that action—not litigation—was needed. Demonstrations and other protests—at first non-violent—became the leading tactic. In the later sixties violence appeared to many to be necessary to achieve equality. The Black Panther organization typified the blacks' willingness to meet violence with violence.

The responses of white America have also been influenced by the many sides of equality. The courts have moved away from what has been labelled "Southern Justice," and both state and federal jurists have, with few exceptions, accepted legal equality. The Supreme Court itself has remained in the center of the struggle for equality. Congress, although reluctantly and following Presidential leadership, enacted Civil Rights laws in 1957, 1960, 1964, and 1968. State and local communities have in some areas passed open housing ordinances. However, several elements of white America have reacted with anger and violence. White Citizen's Councils, states' rights groups, and many individuals have seen a threat to their status and have responded to that threat with forceful talk and action. The presidential campaign of George C. Wallace in 1968 seemed to bring together those who feared all that the Supreme Court decision of 14 years earlier seemed to imply; ten million people responded with approval to Wallace's denunciation of most of the ideas the Court had stood for.

In a narrow sense all these reactions cannot be attributed directly to the Supreme Court. However, *Brown* and the cases which followed from it are part of the struggle for equality raging in America. The Court's decision in *Brown* was a beginning. It was a significant break in the wall of legal discrimination against blacks. For whites it began to illustrate the pervasiveness of a system which had previously remained hidden or ignored. The Court forced unto the public political scene the issue of the role of the black in White America. How can the United States achieve a meaningful society that truly grants equality to all? The answer is far from being evident. In the words of the National Advisory Commission on Civil Disorders:

> Our nation is moving toward two societies, one black and one white— separate and unequal . . . Discrimination and segregation have long permeated much of American life; they now threaten the future of every American.

The following collection of readings illustrates the black–white issue in which the Supreme Court played a crucial role. The web of political forces evolving from the Supreme Court's *Brown* decision—the Second Emancipation Proclamation—is complicated and far reaching. Those forces will be present in America for years to come.

Desegregation: "Separate but Equal Has No Place" (1954)*

Brown v. *Board of Education*

The Justices in the *Brown* decision had to face the formidable precedent of *Plessy* v. *Ferguson*† In 1896, the Court majority had found "the underlying fallacy of the plaintiff's [a Negro] to consist in the assumption that the enforced separation of the two races stamps the colored race with a badge of inferiority. If this be so, it is not by reason of the act, but solely because the colored race chooses to put that construction upon it. . . . If one race be inferior to the other socially, the Constitution . . . cannot put them upon the same plane." In 1954 the Supreme Court was utilizing exactly that Constitution to place the races on an equal plane. Chief Justice Warren delivered the opinion of the Court.

These cases come to us from the States of Kansas, South Carolina, Virginia, and Delaware. . . .

In each of the cases, minors of the Negro race, through their legal representatives, seek the aid of the courts in obtaining admission to

---

*347 U.S. 483.

†163 U.S. 537 (1896).

the public schools of their community on a nonsegregated basis. In each instance, they had been denied admission to schools attended by white children under laws requiring or permitting segregation according to race. This segregation was alleged to deprive the plaintiffs of the equal protection of the laws under the Fourteenth Amendment.

. . . .

Reargument was largely devoted to the circumstances surrounding the adoption of the Fourteenth Amendment in 1868. . . . This discussion and our own investigation convince us that, . . . it is not enough to resolve the problem with which we are faced. At best, they are inconclusive. . . .

An additional reason for the inconclusive nature of the Amendment's history, with respect to segregated schools, is the status of public education at that time. . . . Education of Negroes was almost nonexistent, and practically all of the race were illiterate. . . . Today, in contrast, many Negroes have achieved outstanding success in the arts and sciences as well as in the business and professional world. . . . As a consequence, it is not surprising that there should be so little in the history of the Fourteenth Amendment relating to its intended effect on public education. . . .

In approaching this problem, we cannot turn the clock back to 1868 when the Amendment was adopted, or even to 1896 when *Plessy* v. *Ferguson* was written. We must consider public education in the light of its full development and its present place in American life throughout the Nation. Only in this way can it be determined if segregation in public schools deprives these plaintiffs of the equal protection of the laws.

Today, education is perhaps the most important function of state and local governments. . . . It is the very foundation of good citizenship. Today it is a principal instrument in awakening the child to cultural values, in preparing him for later professional training, and in helping him to adjust normally to his environment. In these days, it is doubtful that any child may reasonably be expected to succeed in life if he is denied the opportunity of an education. Such an opportunity, where the state had undertaken to provide it, is a right which must be made available to all on equal terms.

We come then to the question presented: Does segregation of children in public schools solely on the basis of race, even though the physical facilities and other "tangible" factors may be equal, deprive the children of the minority group of equal educational opportunities? We believe that it does. . . .

"Segregation of white and colored children in public schools has a detrimental effect upon the colored children. The impact is greater when it has the sanction of the law; for the policy of separating the races is usually interpreted as denoting the inferiority of the Negro group. A sense of inferiority affects the motivation of a child to learn. Segregation with the sanction of law, therefore, has a tendency to retard the educational and mental development of Negro children and to deprive them of some of the benefits they would receive in a racially integrated school system." Whatever may have been the extent of psychological knowledge at the time of *Plessy* v. *Ferguson*, this finding is amply supported by modern authority. Any language in *Plessy* v. *Ferguson* contrary to this finding is rejected.

We conclude that in the field of public education the doctrine of "separate but equal" has no place. Separate educational facilities are inherently unequal. Therefore, we hold that the plaintiffs and others similarly situated for whom the actions have been brought are, by reason of the segregation complained of, deprived of the equal protection of the laws guaranteed by the Fourteenth Amendment. . . .

The President Reacts: Eisenhower and Desegregation (1954)*

President Eisenhower was criticized for not strongly supporting the Supreme Court's desegregation decision. The following excerpts from several news conferences subsequent to the *Brown* decision indicate the President's attitude.

HARRY C. DENT (Columbia (S.C.) *State and Record*): Mr. President, do you have any advice to give the South as to just how to react to this recent Supreme Court decision banning segregation, sir?

THE PRESIDENT: Not in the slightest. I thought that Governor Byrnes made a very fine statement when he said, "Let's be calm and let's be reasonable and let's look this thing in the face."

---

*Excerpts from several Presidential news conferences of 1954. Dwight D. Eisenhower, *Public Papers of The President of the United States: 1954* (U.S., Government Printing Office, 1960), pp. 491–492, 700, 1065–1066.

The Supreme Court has spoken and I am sworn to uphold the constitutional processes in this country; and I will obey.

MR. DENT: Mr. President, one more question. Do you think this decision has put Mr. Byrnes and Mr. Byrd and other Southern leaders who supported the Republican ticket in 1952 on the political hotspot, so to speak, since it was brought out under the Republican administration?

THE PRESIDENT: The Supreme Court, as I understand it, is not under any administration.

SARAH McCLENDON (*El Paso Times*): A question along that same line, sir, do you expect that this ruling will, however, alienate many of your Southern supporters politically?

THE PRESIDENT: This is all I will say: I have stood, so far as I know, for honest, decent government since I was first mentioned as a political figure. I am still standing for it, and they will have to make their own decisions as to whether they decide that I have got any sense or haven't.

. . . .

MISS McCLENDON: Sir, have you given any thought to asking Congress for legislation that would enable them to enforce integration in public school education, backing up the Supreme Court decrees?

MR. PRESIDENT: The subject has not even been mentioned to me.

. . . .

MR. DENT: Mr. President, all interested States and groups have now filed their briefs with the Supreme Court as to when and how they would like segregation ended in the public schools, and some have said they want no delay, and others have said they want much delay. And I just wondered if you have your own personal views on that you could give us.

THE PRESIDENT: Not particularly. I will tell you: as you know, the Attorney General is required to file his brief; . . . But the Supreme Court has ruled what is the law in this case, what the Constitution means.

I am sure America wants to obey the Constitution, but there is a very great practical problem involved, and there are certainly deep-seated emotions. What I understand the Supreme Court . . . has undertaken as its task, is to write its orders of procedure in such fashion as to take into consideration these great emotional strains and the practical problems, and try to devise a way where under some form of decentralized process we can bring this about. I don't believe they intend to be arbitrary, at least that is my understanding.

State Courts and Desegregation (1956)*

The North Carolina Supreme Court reaction to the *Brown* decision is typical of most of the courts of Southern states. Although reluctantly, the lower courts followed the precedent of the desegregation ruling.

. . . .

Our deep conviction is that the interpretation now placed on the Fourteenth Amendment, in relation to the right of a state to determine whether children of different races are to be taught in the same or separate public schools, cannot be reconciled with the intent of the framers or ratifiers of the Fourteenth Amendment, the actions of Congress of the United States and of the state legislatures, or the long and consistent judicial interpretation of the Fourteenth Amendment. However that may be, the Constitution of the United States takes precedence over the Constitution of North Carolina. In the interpretation of the Constitution of the United States, the Supreme Court of the United States is final arbiter. Its decision in the *Brown* case is the law of the land and will remain so unless reversed or altered by constitutional means. Recognizing fully that its decision is authoritative in this jurisdiction, any provision of the Constitution or statutes of North Carolina in conflict therewith must be deemed invalid.

"Interposition" and the President (1956) †

WILLIAM V. SHANNON (*New York Post*): As you may know, four of the southern State legislatures have passed interposition resolutions stating that the Supreme Court decision outlawing segregation has no force and effect in their States; and I was wondering what you thought about this concept of interposition, and what you thought was the role of the federal government in enforcing the Supreme Court decision?

THE PRESIDENT: Well, of course, you have asked a very vast question that is filled with argument on both sides. You have raised

---

*Excerpts from *Constantian* v. *Anson County*, 244 N.C. 221, 228–9 (1956).

†Excerpts from President Eisenhower's news conference. Dwight D. Eisenhower, *Public Papers of the President of the United States: 1956*, (U.S.: Government Printing Office, 1960), pp. 269–270.

the question of States rights versus Federal power; you have particularly brought up the question whether the Supreme Court is the last word we have in the interpretation of our Constitution.

Now, this is what I say: there are adequate legal means of determining all of these factors. The Supreme Court has issued its own operational directives and delegated power to the district courts.

I expect that we are going to make progress, and the Supreme Court itself said it does not expect revolutionary action suddenly executed. We will make progress, and I am not going to attempt to tell them how it is going to be done.

.   .   .   .

The Southern Manifesto: Declaration of Constitutional Principles (1956)*

The Manifesto of 96 Congressmen, printed below, represented the concerns and desires of perhaps the majority of Southern leaders in the years following the desegregation ruling.

The unwarranted decision of the Supreme Court in the public school cases is now bearing the fruit always produced when men substitute naked power for established law.

The Founding Fathers gave us a Constitution of checks and balances because they realized the inescapable lesson of history that no man or group of men can be safely entrusted with unlimited power. They framed this Constitution with its provisions for change by amendment in order to secure the fundamentals of government against the dangers of temporary popular passion or the personal predilections of public office-holders.

We regard the decision of the Supreme Court in the school cases as a clear abuse of judicial power. It climaxes a trend in the Federal Judiciary undertaking to legislate, in derogation of the authority of Congress, and to encroach upon the reserved rights of the States and the people.

The original Constitution does not mention education. Neither does the Fourteenth Amendment nor any other amendment. . . .

.   .   .   .

---

*Congressional Record, March 12, 1956, pp. 4460–4461, 4515–4516.

In the case of *Plessy* v. *Ferguson* in 1896 the Supreme Court expressly declared that under the Fourteenth Amendment no person was denied any of his rights if the States provided separate but equal public facilities. This decision has been followed in many other cases. . . .

This interpretation, restated time and again, became a part of the life of the people of many of the States and confirmed their habits, customs, traditions, and way of life. It is founded on elemental humanity and common sense, for parents should not be deprived by Government of the right to direct the lives and education of their own children. . . .

This unwarranted exercise of power by the Court, contrary to the Constitution, is creating chaos and confusion in the States principally affected. It is destroying the amicable relations between the white and Negro races that have been created through ninety years of patient effort by the good people of both races. It has planted hatred and suspicion where there has been heretofore friendship and understanding.

Without regard to the consent of the governed, outside agitators are threatening immediate and revolutionary changes in our public-school systems. If done, this is certain to destroy the system of public education in some of the States.

With the gravest concern for the explosive and dangerous condition created by this decision and inflamed by outside meddlers:

We reaffirm our reliance on the Constitution as the fundamental law of the land.

We decry the Supreme Court's encroachments on rights reserved to the States and to the people, contrary to established law, and to the Constitution.

We commend the motives of those States which have declared the intention to resist forced integration by any lawful means.

We appeal to the States and people who are not directly affected by these decisions to consider the constitutional principles involved against the time when they too, on issues vital to them, may be the victims of judicial encroachment.

.   .   .   .

We pledge ourselves to use all lawful means to bring about a reversal of this decision which is contrary to the Constitution and to prevent the use of force in its implementation.

In this trying period, as we all seek to right this wrong we appeal to our people not to be provoked by the agitators and troublemakers invading our States and to scrupulously refrain from disorder and lawless acts. . . .

The President and the Southern Manifesto (1956)*

In reaction to criticisms regarding his reluctance to push for desegregation and in response to the Southern Manifesto, President Eisenhower appealed for patience and moderation.

EDWARD P. MORGAN (American Broadcasting Company): Mr.
President, southern members of Congress, including a couple of Re-
publicans, have posed a direct challenge to both the other branches
of Government, first, in the implied if not declared threat to block
your appointments to the judiciary, which might find disfavor on the
racial issue; and, second, in a manifesto which was introduced in
Congress on Monday, in which some 100 members of the House and
Senate commit themselves to try to overturn the Supreme Court decision on segregation. Would you comment on those developments,
sir, particularly with reference to what you think the Executive
responsibility is and should be?

THE PRESIDENT: Well, you are asking a question that we are
probably going to be busy on for a while.

First, I have nothing whatsoever to say about their right to confirm or not confirm. The constitutional duty of the Senate to act as
it sees fit upon the nominations sent up by the President is clear.

. . . .

Now, the first thing about the manifesto is this: that they say
they are going to use every legal means. No one in any responsible
position anywhere has talked nullification; there would be a place
where we get to a very bad spot for the simple reason I am sworn to
defend and uphold the Constitution of the United States and, of
course, I can never abandon or refuse to carry out my own duty.

Let us remember that the Supreme Court itself talked about
emotionalism in this question, and it was for that reason that it said,
"Progress must be gradual."

Now, let us not forget there has been some progress. I believe there
is something on the order of more than a quarter of a million of Negro
children in the border and some southern States, that have been in-

---

*Excerpts from President Eisenhower's news conference. Dwight D. Eisenhower,
Public Papers of the President of the United States: 1956 (U.S.: Government Printing
Office, 1960), pp. 303–305.

tegrated in the schools, and except for a certain area in which the difficulties are greatest, there has been progress.

.   .   .   .

So, let us remember that there are people who are ready to approach this thing with moderation, but with the determination to make the progress that the Supreme Court asked for.

If ever there was a time when we must be patient without being complacent, when we must be understanding of other people's deep emotions as well as our own, this is it. Extremists on neither side are going to help this situation, and we can only believe that the good sense, the common sense, of Americans will bring this thing along. The length of time I am not even going to talk about; I don't know anything about the length of time it will take.

We are not talking here about coercing, using force in a general way; we are simply going to uphold the Constitution of the United States, see that the progress as ordered by them is carried out.

Now, let us remember this one thing, and it is very important: the people who have this deep emotional reaction on the other side were not acting over these past three generations in defiance of law. They were acting in compliance with the law as interpreted by the Supreme Court of the United States under the decision of 1896. (*Plessy* v. *Ferguson*.)

Now, that has been completely reversed, and it is going to take time for them to adjust their thinking and their progress to that. But I have never yet given up my belief that the American people, faced with a great problem like this, will approach it intelligently and with patience and with understanding, and we will get somewhere; and I do deplore any great extreme action on either side.

.   .   .   .

The NAACP versus the 48 States (1958)*

Two months after the Senate confirmed the Chief Justice's appointment, on May 17, 1954, the Warren Supreme Court issued its revolutionary decision (*Brown* v. *Board of Education*)—a unanimous one—in the school-segregation cases.

---

*Reprinted from Rosalie M. Gordon, *Nine Men Against America* (New York: The Devin-Adair Company, 1960) with permission from the publisher.

What the Court did in that decision was not to settle the issue of segregation or integration of Negro and white pupils in the public schools. Racial issues are not settled by law—constitutional or otherwise. They are settled by time and the forbearance and patience of the people involved. One of the major human tragedies resulting from the Court's decision is that an issue that was well on its way to solution—slowly, to be sure, in some places—will now plague us for many years to come, intensified almost beyond reason by the Court's action.

But since ours is meant to be a government of law and not of men, the overwhelming tragedy for us all is that the Court, in its segregation decision, stormed one of those last remaining bastions of a free people we have previously mentioned—the locally controlled and supported public-school systems of the sovereign states. For, by that decision the Supreme Court handed to the central government a power it had never before possessed—the power to put its grasping and omnipotent hand into a purely local function. If the federal government can tell the public school in your town—whether in a northern, southern, western, or eastern state—who it shall or shall not admit, the next step is as logical as that winter follows fall. It will not be long before the socialist revolutionaries will have what they want—control by the central government of what to teach and what not to teach, how to teach it and how not to teach it in the public schools of America.

The legal defendants in the school cases were a few Southern states. But the real defendants were each and every one of the 48 sovereign states of the American Union and the Constitution they established for their own government.

The plaintiff who brought the cases before the Supreme Court is an organization known as the National Association for the Advancement of the Colored People (NAACP). It is a fairly old organization which started out with the avowed purpose of securing justice for Negroes who were discriminated against because of their race. But in the last decade or two, coincident with the rising wave of left-wing activity in America, it has become extremely militant.

. . . .

The Supreme Court Makes a Law

In order to bring about this revolution of totalitarian proportions, it was necessary for Chief Justice Warren and his colleagues to ignore 165 years of Supreme Court history and a decision of the Court that had stood unchallenged for nearly 60 years.

In 1896 a case (*Plessy* v. *Ferguson*) came before the Court involving a state law. Louisiana had a statute providing for segregation of races on railroad trains. The law was challenged on the ground that it violated the Fourteenth Amendment to the Constitution. The Supreme Court decided that, since the Louisiana law provided for "separate but equal" facilities, it was not in violation of the Constitution. The problem of segregating or not segregating the races was a state problem. The State of Louisiana, exercising its sovereign function, passed a law providing for segregation. The only question to be settled by the Court was whether or not the law violated any provision of the Constitution. The Court did not say to Louisiana: you must segregate, or you must not segregate. It simply said that because the Louisiana law, while providing for segregation, also provided for separate but equal facilities, Louisiana had fulfilled her obligation under the Fourteenth Amendment to the Constitution.

Actually, this was not the first, or the last, time the question came before the Court. It arose at least six separate times in a period of 75 years. And each time the Supreme Court upheld the doctrine of equal but separate facilities.

. . . .

Faced with a body of law and precedent like this, what was the Warren Supreme Court to do? It did something unprecedented in our history. It threw out the window the Constitution and all previous Court interpretations, and arrogated to itself a function reserved only for our representatives in Congress. It wrote a new law—something the Supreme Court has no right to do—and proclaimed it the law of the land by judicial fiat. The Congress of the United States—the only body to which the Constitution gives law-making powers—has never passed a law forcing the races to be mixed in the public schools. If it had, it would then have been up to the Supreme Court to say whether the law was constitutional or not. In the light of our past constitutional and judicial history, a lawful Court would have had to declare such a law unconstitutional, since it would be an obvious invasion by the Congress of a purely state function.

But the Warren Court did what Justice Black (who concurred) had once accused President Truman of doing—it usurped the legislative function of the Congress. It wrote a law—a law based on the very doubtful psycho-sociological precept that if the races went to separate schools, it would retard the development of the Negro children. Dr. Pitirim A. Sorokin, one of our most distinguished students of sociology, has said of this combination of sociology and psychology that both "are in a blind alley of subjective and evanescent hearsay trivia. In our courts most of this 'hearsay stuff' is rejected as evidence." But not in the Supreme Court of the United States. It wrote a law based on this pseudo-science of "hearsay trivia." It said that Negro children would be retarded in their development if they were not mixed with white children in the schools because this "generates a feeling of inferiority as to their status." Those are the Court's words.

Interposition by The States (1960)*

Typical of the reactions of State legislatures is the following interposition resolution of Louisiana. States' Rights became the issue for many of the Southern States. Despite such actions the Constitution of the United States remained the supreme law of the land and the Supreme Court remained that document's final interpreter.

An act to interpose the sovereignty of the State of Louisiana against the unlawful encroachments by the judicial and executive branches of the Federal Government in the operation of public schools of the State of Louisiana, which constitute a deliberate, palpable and dangerous exercise of governmental powers not granted to the United States by the United States Constitution; to prohibit all officers, agents and persons acting under orders of the federal courts or any other branch of the Federal Government from interfering with the maintenance of any State public school, or any officer, agent or employee of the State or any subdivision of the State engaged in the maintenance of such schools or in carrying out the provisions of this Act, or other law, right or power of the State of Louisiana under its reserved powers provided by the Tenth Amendment to the United States Constitution; and to provide penalties for violations hereof.

. . . .

Whereas, contrary to its well ordered line of decisions in 1896 (*Plessy* vs. *Ferguson*, 163 U.S. 550) affirming all prior federal and state court decisions in point, and repeatedly until 1950 (339 U.S. 629 and 639), that the Fourteenth Amendment did not prohibit the

*From: *Race Relations Law Reporter* (Vol. III, 1960) pp. 1177–1182.

States, in the exercise of their police power, from providing separate but equal facilities for different races by the establishment of separate schools for white and colored children, and "the education of the people in schools maintained by state taxation is a matter belonging to the respective states, and any interference on the part of the federal authority with the management of such schools cannot be justified" (175 U.S. 528), and contrary to the fact that the same Congress which submitted the Joint Resolution for the Fourteenth Amendment had passed an Act for segregated schools in the District of Columbia, which is under its jurisdiction; and contrary to the fact that the same court held and reaffirmed in scores of cases since 1837 (36 U.S. 648, 113 U.S. 27) that no provision of the United States Constitution and none of the Amendments added to that instrument was intended or designed to interfere with the police power of the various States to prescribe regulations to promote the health, peace, morals, education and good order of the people, the United States Supreme Court, in *Brown* vs. *Topeka*, and consolidated cases, rendered a decision on May 17, 1954 (347 U.S. 483) repudiating the Fourteenth Amendment as having no intended effect on public education, and stating it could not "turn the clock back to 1868 when the Amendment was adopted, or even to 1896" when the *Plessy* vs. *Ferguson* decision was written by it (holding that the Fourteenth Amendment did not prohibit States from operating separate public schools for white and Negro children), because, "whatever may have been the extent of psychological knowledge at the time of *Plessy* vs. *Ferguson* (1896) this finding is amply supported by modern authority," and citing as its 1954 modern "psychological" authority, not any provision of the Constitution or Act of Congress enacted pursuant thereto, but books written by various persons whose memberships in communist and subversive organizations dedicated to the overthrow of the United States government and the Constitution were matters of public record in the files of Congress and the Department of Justice, and easily available to the members of the Court, and in its decree in said *Brown* vs. *Topeka* case (349 U.S. 294) the Supreme Court directed all lower federal courts to render unlawful orders to compel all state public schools in the country to racially integrate "with all deliberate speed."

. . . .

Whereas, further evidence of the deliberate, palpable and dangerous usurpation of ungranted power and its violation of the United States Constitution is shown by the fact that the United States Supreme Court cited as authority for its decision in the *Brown* vs. *Topeka* consolidated cases so-called modern authority, or books on psychology and sociology which had not been offered in evidence during trials of said cases, . . . and the very use of such books as authority for its decision in said case, without opportunity to the defendants to examine or rebut has been consistently held by the same Court in its previous decisions to constitute a denial of the fundamentals of a trial, and a denial of "due process of law" in violation of the Fifth Amendment of the Constitution, and would be condemnation without trial.

Whereas, forced racial integration of public schools by the Federal Government in Washington, District of Columbia, as reported after investigation by the Committee on the District of Columbia of the House of Representatives, 84th Congress, 2nd Session, 1957, results in continual disturbances of the peace, acts of violence, thefts, immoral conduct on the part of Negro boys against white girls and Negro girls' immoral propositions to white boys, assaults and rapes by Negroes of white school girls and teachers, which caused a marked lowering of educational standards, and which also caused an exodus of a large part of the white population from the District of Columbia to avoid such a situation against the best interest of the health, peace, morals, education and good order of the people; all of which is the duty of and within the sole power of the state to protect and promote against unlawful usurpations by the Federal Government.

. . . .

. . . . therefore:

Section 1

That by substituting the current political and social philosophy of its members to unsettle the great constitutional principles so clearly established, the federal courts destroyed the stability of the Constitution and usurped the power of Congress to submit, and of the several states to approve, constitutional changes as required by the Constitution. . . .

Section 2

That the decision of the United States Supreme Court in the case of *Brown* v. *Topeka Board of Education,* on May 17, 1954, constitutes a deliberate, palpable and dangerous attempt to change the true intent and meaning of the Constitution, and said decision itself is unconstitutional and in violation of the Fourteenth Amendment, and it thereby establishes a judicial precedent, if allowed to stand, for the ultimate destruction of constitutional government.

Section 3

That the States have never delegated to the United States government, nor to any branch of that government, the power to change the Constitution nor have they surrendered to the Federal Government the power to prohibit to the States the right to maintain racially separate public school facilities or the right to determine when such facilities are in the best interest of their citizens, nor have the States surrendered to the Federal Government the State's police power to prescribe regulations to promote the health, peace, morals, education and good order of the people.

.   .   .   .

Section 6

That no governmental agency, judge, marshal or other officer, agent or employee of the United States shall undertake or attempt the enforcement of any judgment, decree or order of any Federal Court, nor to make or attempt to make service of any citation, summons, warrant or process in connection therewith, predicated upon the United States Supreme Court's decision and decree in the case of *Brown* vs. *Topeka Board of Education,* upon any officer of the State of Louisiana, or of any of its subdivisions, agencies or School Boards, or upon any of their agents, employees or representatives in the maintenance of the public schools of the State, or who may be engaged in carrying out the provisions of this Act, or other law, right or power of the State of Louisiana under its reserved powers provided by the Tenth Amendment to the United States Constitution.

.   .   .   .

Section 8

That the people of this State feel, as they ever have, the most sincere affection for the people of the other States of the Union, and the most scrupulous fidelity to the Constitution which is the pledge of mutual friendship, and this Legislature solemnly appeals to the like dispositions of the other States, in confidence that they will concur with the State in declaring, as it does hereby declare, that the aforesaid decisions are unconstitutional, and that the necessary and proper measures will be taken by each for cooperating with this State, in maintaining unimpaired the authorities, rights and liberties, reserved to the States respectively, or to the people.

.   .   .   .

The Talmadge Amendment (1960)*

Herman E. Talmadge

In an attempt to overturn *Brown* v. *Board of Education,* Senator Talmadge (D., Ga.), along with other southern senators, proposed a constitutional amendment restoring full control of educational systems to the state and local school groups. Although failing to achieve any substantial support from his colleagues, Talmadge's effort was typical of Southern leaders.

Notwithstanding any other provision of the Constitution, every state shall have exclusive control of its public schools, public educational institutions, and public educational systems, whether operated by the state, or by political or other subdivisions of the state, or by instrumentalities or agencies of the state; provided, however, that nothing contained in this Article shall be construed to authorize any religious belief, the right to attend schools equal, in respect to the quality and ability of the teachers, curriculum, and physical facilities, to those attended by other pupils attending schools in the same school system.

Educational Problems of Public Schools (1962) †

Dean John H. Fischer

Obviously the desegregation of schools involves problems far beyond the Constitutional question itself. In the following speech, Dean John H. Fischer of Teachers College, Columbia University, outlines several guides for administrators and teachers.

To say that the problems of race relations in the United States are complex hardly helps to clarify our situation, but unless the complexity

---

*From *Congressional Record,* January 28, 1960, 1499–1500.

†Reprinted with permission from *Vital Speeches* (May 15, 1962). Speech was delivered by Dean Fischer at the Fourth Annual Conference of the Commission on Civil Rights in May, 1962.

of this matter is seen and taken constantly into account, no single step is likely to be very useful. The problems of American education are no less complex. In a nation as diversified as ours, universal education can never be simple, and it is universal education, with emphasis on both adjective and noun, that we must now achieve. As the issues of race relations permeate almost every aspect of our life, so events in our schools are interlaced with virtually everything we do or hope to do. The difficulties of operating schools which can cope successfully and, as they must, simultaneously with both racial and educational issues are therefore among the most puzzling of all the problems facing the American people.

.   .   .   .

The temptation is always strong to say that the Negro child should be seen merely as any other child, respected as an individual, and provided with an educational program that will best meet his particular combination of needs. Of course the Negro child, like every other child, is entitled to be treated as an individual. Such treatment is the only sound basis for projecting his or any other child's education, but the easy generalization does not always come to grips with the whole truth.

The American Negro youngster happens to be a member of a large and distinctive group that for a very long time has been the object of special political, legal, and social action. This, I remind you, is not a question of what should be true, or might have been, but an undeniable and inescapable fact. To act as though any child is suddenly separable from his history is indefensible. In terms of educational planning, it is also irresponsible.

Every Negro child is the victim of the history of his race in this country. On the day he enters kindergarten, he carries a burden no white child can ever know, no matter what other handicaps or disabilities he may suffer. We are dealing here with no ordinary question of intercultural understanding, although admittedly cultural difference is a part of the difficulty. Nor are we concerned with only the usual range of psycho-educational problems, for the psychological situation of the Negro child is affected by quite special social considerations.

.   .   .   .

Many of the recent efforts to integrate Negro pupils into the mainstream of American public education have been built on the assumption that the problems are essentially administrative, legal, or political. As a consequence, we have seen drives for what is called "open enrollment" and other schemes to bring about, usually through directive action, a desired combination of races in particular classrooms or schools. Having worked in school administration for some twenty-seven years, I claim some knowledge of at least its limitations. Although, as you might suspect, I hold that administrative procedures and actions can be useful in education, I grow steadily more certain that no major problem of education—by which I mean really effective teaching and learning—has ever been solved solely, or even primarily, by legal or administrative action. To be sure, such action often lays the necessary groundwork and provides the setting in which good teachers may carry on their work, but the critical point in any educational system is found ultimately in the relation between the teacher and the pupil.

What, then, can be done to produce the sort of pupil-teacher relationship that will contribute most to the tasks we are thinking of today?

For one thing, we must continue to recognize the element of cultural difference. As the Educational Policies Commission pointed out in a recent statement, a principal part of the difficulty of what the Commission calls the "disadvantaged American" is the fact that a substantial minority of Americans have grown up in cultures which are not compatible with much of modern life. This minority consists by no means only of Negroes, nor are all Negroes culturally disadvantaged. But vast numbers of them are, as a direct consequence of legal and social segregation.

.   .   .   .

In dealing with a population which is racially and culturally integrated, the school must begin by encouraging teachers to understand the special factors in the backgrounds of all their children, to take these differences imaginatively into account, and to build curricula and teaching techniques that reflect not only idealism but realism as well.

In addition to the cultural aspect, intellectual competence, many Negro children face special problems that should be better understood than they often are. Obviously many Americans of Negro ancestry have attained distinction in fields requiring intellectual eminence and millions of others daily apply their minds with excellent results in more humble ways. . . . The fact remains that during years of oppression, first under slavery and later under more subtle forms of discrimination, the opportunities for large numbers of Negroes to apply their own rational powers with initiative and freedom to important problems have been far more limited than the opportunities available to other racial groups. Many Negro children, therefore, carry the disabling scars of the culture in which they were nurtured, a culture which encouraged the use of muscles and not only discouraged but often penalized those who sought to use their minds creatively. The school must take all of this into account and build programs and provide opportunities which not only reflect these facts but move aggressively to compensate for them.

Every educational problem has its emotional side, and the special problems of educating Negro children in desegregated schools have theirs. . . .

One of the most serious of the details is the problem of motivation. The Horatio Alger story is a well established part of our folklore, but few Americans would argue that the typical Alger hero would have made it had his skin been of a darker shade. The sense of frustration which any minority child may experience is heightened in the case of the Negro child, who discovers all too early that his minority has both a special history in the United States and quite unique problems. As a consequence, his attitude toward himself and toward his racial group complicates the effort to help him secure an adequate education. In some cases, he may rationalize his failures by attributing them to limitations which do not, in fact, exist for him. In others, he may develop an understandable aggressiveness which will neither compensate for external difficulties nor correct his own shortcomings. The wise and well-informed teacher is aware of these emotional complications and undertakes to deal with them in positive ways.

In the face of these facts, and in the light of our democratic values, what guidelines for policy and practice in the conduct of American public schools are implied?

In the first place, it is essential to emphasize on every possible occasion and in everything we do in schools that the rights of students, the assessment of their needs, and the release of their potentialities must be approached on an individual basis.

.   .   .   .

A second guideline for the development of policy and practice centers about the concept of equality of opportunity. "Equality of opportunity," as we customarily use the phrase, means much more than a schoolroom desk for every child. It connotes, rather, a condition in which every American may rightfully expect to find himself in fair competition with every other American. This condition is achieved and maintained by the operation of a host of agencies and forces, some political, some social, others economic or cultural. The public school has never been the only agency concerned with producing equality of opportunity, but its role is fundamental to the total effort.

.   .   .   .

A third guide to educational policy and practice seems relevant to this discussion. If we are to keep the focus of our educational effort on the welfare of the individual child, we shall do well to avoid what is sometimes called social engineering. The very term is inconsistent with the purposes and values of democracy. Even the most desirable end does not justify manipulating people to create a structure pleasing to some master planner.

. . . .

Desegregation of Public Education: Civil Rights Act of 1964

Ten years after the *Brown* case, Congress, upon the initiative of the President, passed the Civil Rights Act of 1964 which included provisions whereby the Attorney General would institute civil suits in the name of the United States to force compliance with the *Brown* decision. Title VI provides further compliance by the withdrawal of federal assistance to those school districts that are not desegregating "with all deliberate speed."

Title IV

Section 407. (a) *Whenever the Attorney General receives a complaint in writing—*

(1) signed by a parent or group of parents to the effect that his or their minor children, as members of a class of persons similarly situated, are being deprived by a school board of the equal protection of the laws, or

(2) signed by an individual, or his parent, to the effect that he has been denied admission to or not permitted to continue in attendance at a public college by reason of race, color, religion, or national origin, and the Attorney General believes the complaint is meritorious and certifies that the signer or signers of such complaint are unable, in his judgment, to initiate and maintain appropriate legal proceedings for relief and that the institution of an action will materially further the orderly achievement of desegregation in public education, the Attorney General is authorized, after giving notice of such complaint to the appropriate school board or college authority and after certifying that he is satisfied that such board or authority has had a reasonable time to adjust the conditions alleged in such complaint, to institute for or in the name of the court of the United States a civil action in any appropriate district court of the United States against

such parties and for such relief as may be appropriate, and such court shall have and shall exercise jurisdiction of proceedings instituted pursuant to this section, provided that nothing herein shall empower any official or court of the United States to issue any order seeking to achieve a racial balance in any school by requiring the transportation of pupils or students from one school to another or one school district to another in order to achieve such racial balance, or otherwise enlarge the existing power of the court to insure compliance with constitutional standards.

. . . .

Title VI

Section 601. No person in the United States shall, on the ground of race, color, or national origin, be excluded from participation in, be denied the benefits of, or be subjected to discrimination under any program or activity receiving Federal financial assistance.

Section 602. Each Federal department and agency which is empowered to extend Federal financial assistance to any program or activity, by way of grant, loan, or contract other than a contract of insurance or guaranty, is authorized and directed to effectuate the provisions of section 601 with respect to such program or activity, ... Compliance with any requirement adopted pursuant to this section may be effected (1) by the termination of or refusal to grant or to continue assistance under such program or activity to any recipient as to whom there has been an express finding on the record, after opportunity for hearing, of a failure to comply with such requirement, ...

Ten Years Later: Prince Edward County, Virginia (1964)*

Griffin v. *County School Board of Prince Edward County*

Ten years after the *Brown* decision only about ten percent of the black students in the South were attending desegregated facilities. The school board of Prince Edward County, Virginia, closed its public

---

*377 U.S. 218 (1964).

schools in order to avoid compliance with the *Brown* edict. Private schools were set up for the white children, but the 1,700 black children in the County went without schooling. The following case voided such action. Justice Black delivered the opinion of the Court.

We agree with the District Court that, under the circumstances here, closing the Prince Edward County Schools while public schools in all the other counties of Virginia were being maintained, denied the petitioners and the class of Negro students they represent, the equal protection of the laws guaranteed by the Fourteenth Amendment. . . .

Since 1959, all Virginia counties have had the benefits of public schools but one: Prince Edward. . . .

Virginia law, as here applied, unquestionably treats the school children of Prince Edward differently from the way it treats the school children of all other Virginia counties. Prince Edward children must go to a private school or none at all; all the other Virginia children can go to public schools. Closing Prince Edward's schools bears more heavily on Negro children in Prince Edward County since white children there have accredited private schools which they can attend, while colored children until very recently have had no available private schools, and even the school they now attend is a temporary expedient. Apart from this expedient, the result is that Prince Edward County school children, if they go to school in their own county, must go to racially segregated schools which, although designated as private, are beneficiaries of county and state support.

. . . .

The record in the present case could not be clearer that Prince Edward's public schools were closed and private schools operated in their place with state and county assistance, for one reason, and one reason only: to ensure, through measures taken by the county and the State, that white and colored children in Prince Edward County would not, under any circumstances, go to the same school. Whatever nonracial grounds might support a State's allowing a county to abandon public schools, the object must be a constitutional one, and grounds of race and opposition to desegregation do not qualify as constitutional. . . .

Accordingly, we agree with the District Court that closing the Prince Edward schools and meanwhile contributing to the support of the private segregated white schools that took their place denied petitioners the equal protection of the laws. . . .

School Segregation a Live Issue 15 Years After High Court Ban (1969)*

Fifteen years after the Supreme Court held public school segregation to be unconstitutional, nationwide controversy rages over how—and in some areas whether—the decision should be carried out.

. . . .

Much progress has been made toward eliminating the dual school system that existed in 17 Southern and Border States and the District of Columbia when the decision was handed down on May 17, 1954.

But the dual system has persisted in many counties and cities of the South, and in the North there has been a vast increase in de facto segregation. The federal authorities believe racial separation in classrooms is now about equal North and South.

Now, observers believe, the struggle is at a particularly crucial point. The Nixon Administration has not yet demonstrated how hard it will push to eliminate what is left of the dual system that had existed by law, or to reverse the trend to segregated schools in Northern cities.

At the same time, the separatist movement that has developed among blacks in the last five years has diminished the drive for desegregation. Many Negroes now declare integration to be either irrelevant or undesirable.

A particularly ominous sign is the rise in violence this year in inner city schools as Negroes have demanded black studies, community control and other changes in the system.

However, on the fifteenth anniversary of the decision the essential question in all regions of the country is what to do about the black schools that have failed to achieve the kind of education that both white and Negro parents want for their children.

One irony of the struggle is that, although the decision is widely believed to have prompted the Negro revolution, there have been fewer quantitative gains for blacks in integrated education than in other areas such as employment, public accommodations and voter registration.

Another irony is that rural Clarendon County in the South Carolina lowlands, so untypical of the rest of America, can provide an example of what is involved nationally, even in the Northern cities.

. . . .

*©1967–1969 by the New York Times Company. Reprinted with permission from *New York Times*, May 17, 1969, pp. 1, 40.

On the tenth anniversary of the Court decision, nothing had changed in Clarendon County. The original desegregation decree was never served by the Federal District Court and the National Association for the Advancement of Colored People, which brought the original suit, several years later went back to the court with a new case.

In the last two to three years the white schools of the county submitted peacefully to token integration under court orders and the county is now receiving full Federal funds.

In the town of Summerton, there are more than 200 whites and 24 Negroes in a former white school. When integration came 110 whites left the public school system and are now attending a private school called the Clarendon Hall Academy. There are no whites in the Negro school. This is the pattern throughout the county.

. . . .

The plaintiffs in the Clarendon County case are now asking that one county high school be built for both races and that existing buildings be used as grammar and junior high centers on a zoned attendance basis. The ratio would then be about three blacks to one white in the high school.

This has been done in a number of Southern communities where Negroes do not make up the majority. But in Clarendon County, it could be expected to cause most whites to transfer to private schools.

In desegregation matters, the courts in recent years have been following the lead of the Department of Health, Education and Welfare. Nixon Administration officials have said that they will enforce the law but do not intend to let desegregation destroy the public schools. This portends continual delay in eradicating inferior centers like the Manning Training School.

The winds of change have begun to be felt in education here, but only indirectly as a result of the 1954 decision. The Voting Rights Act of 1965 increased Negro registration until there are now almost as many black voters as white.

Consequently, in 1968 the white public officials agreed to help sponsor a Headstart center sought by the black community. Before the Office of Economic Opportunity would fund the center, however, it insisted that the center have white students as well as black.

. . . .

What desegregation has been achieved in the nation's public schools has resulted from the combined pressures of the Federal courts, acting under the 1954 decision, and the executive branch, enforcing Title VI of the Civil Rights Act of 1964. That section of the law, which flowed from the court decision, bans racial discrimination in any federally assisted program.

Compliance was slow in the 1950's and the early sixties and was marred by constitutional crises and violence, such as those at the Little Rock, Arkansas, high school in 1957 and at the University of Mississippi in 1962.

Almost eighty percent of the Negro students were still attending Negro schools. Many of these had undergone some faculty integration, as required by the Federal department, but educators say most of them, like Manning Training School, have not greatly improved.

About 120 school districts in the Deep South—most with large Negro populations—had been found to be out of compliance with Title VI and were not receiving Federal funds. About 364 districts were under court desegregation orders.

In a number of Northern cities, desegregation has been achieved by voluntary efforts, but this is the exception. North and South, officials say, the black schools are shunned by almost everyone.

Enforcement of Desegregation (1969)*

Robert H. Finch and John N. Mitchell

Under Title VI of the Civil Rights Act of 1964 the Federal Government could withhold funds from public schools which had not sufficiently desegregated. In the spring of 1965 the Johnson administration issued a set of guidelines, designating 1967 as the final date of total compliance with the *Brown* decision. The deadline was subsequently extended until September, 1968. In January, 1968 the President set the "final deadline" for September, 1969 for all districts except those with extreme problems which had until 1970. The following statement by Secretary of Health, Education and Welfare Finch and Attorney General Mitchell spells out the Nixon Administration's approach to desegregation. "Limited delay" appears to be possible again.

This Administration is unequivocally committed to the goal of finally ending racial discrimination in schools, steadily and speedily,

*New York Times, July 4, 1969, p. 7.

in accordance with the law of the land. The new procedures set forth in this statement are designed to achieve that goal in a way that will improve, rather than disrupt, the education of the children concerned.

The time has come to face the facts involved in solving this difficult problem and to strip away the confusion which has too often characterized discussion of this issue. Setting, breaking and resetting unrealistic "deadlines" may give the appearance of great Federal activity, but in too many cases it has actually impeded progress.

.   .   .   .

Fifteen years have passed since the Supreme Court, in *Brown* v. *Board of Education*, declared that racially segregated public schools are inherently unequal, and that officially imposed segregation is in violation of the Constitution. Fourteen years have passed since the Court, in its second *Brown* decision, recognized the tenacious and deep-rooted nature of the problems that would have to be overcome, but nevertheless ordered that school authorities should proceed toward full compliance "with all deliberate speed."

Progress toward compliance has been orderly and uneventful in some areas, and marked by bitterness and turmoil in others. Efforts to achieve compliance have been a process of trial and error, occasionally accompanied by unnecessary friction, and sometimes resulting in a temporary—but for those affected, irremediable—sacrifice in the quality of education.

Some friction is inevitable. Some disruption of education is inescapable. Our aim is to achieve full compliance with the law in a manner that provides the most progress with the least disruption and friction.

.   .   .   .

In last year's landmark *Green* case, the Supreme Court noted: "There is no universal answer to the complex problems of desegregation; there is obviously no one plan that will do the job in every case. The matter must be assessed in light of the circumstances present and the options available in each instance." As recently as this past May, in *Montgomery* v. *Carr*, the Court also noted that "in this field the way must always be left open for experimentation."

Accordingly, it is not our purpose here to lay down a single arbitrary date by which the desegregation process should be completed in all districts, or to lay down a single, arbitrary system by which it should be achieved.

A policy requiring all school districts, regardless of the difficulties they face, to complete desegregation by the same terminal date is too rigid to be either workable or equitable. This is reflected in the history of the "guidelines."

After passage of the 1964 Civil Rights Act, an HEW policy statement first interpreted the act to require affirmative steps to end racial discrimination in all districts within one year of the act's effective date. When this deadline was not achieved, a new deadline was set for 1967. When this in turn was not met, the deadline was moved to the 1968 school year, or at the latest 1969. This, too, was later modified, administratively, to provide a 1970 deadline for districts with a majority Negro population, or for those in which new construction necessary for desegregation was scheduled for early completion.

Our policy in this area will be as defined in the latest Supreme Court and circuit court decisions: that school districts not now in compliance are required to complete the process of desegregation "at the earliest practicable date"; that "the time for mere 'deliberate speed' has run out"; and, in the words of *Green*, that "the burden on a school board today is to come forward with a plan that promises realistically to work, and promises realistically to work now."

.   .   .   .

In general, such a plan must provide for full compliance now— that is, the "terminal date" must be the 1969–70 school year. In some districts there may be sound reasons for some limited delay. In considering whether and how much additional time is justified, we will take into account only bona fide educational and administrative problems. Examples of such problems would be serious shortages of necessary physical facilities, financial resources or faculty. Additional time will be allowed only where those requesting it sustain the heavy factual burden of proving that compliance with the 1969–70 time schedule cannot be achieved; where additional time is allowed, it will be the minimum shown to be necessary.

Chapter Two

Rights of the Accused:
The Supreme Court and the Criminal

No person shall . . . be compelled in any criminal case to be a witness
against himself, nor be deprived of life, liberty and property without
due process of law. . . .

Fifth Amendment to
U.S. Constitution

In all criminal prosecutions, the accused shall . . . have the Assistance of Counsel for his defence.

Sixth Amendment to
U.S. Constitution

Although not limited to these Amendments, the revolution in the
rights of the accused has derived primarily from the Supreme Court's
emphasis on the "right to remain silent" and the "right to counsel"
aspects of the Bill of Rights. Through selective incorporation of these
provisions into the due process clause of the Fourteenth Amendment,
the states have been compelled to observe the dictates of the Bill of
Rights.

Lost sometimes in the political responses to the Supreme Court's
decisions concerning rights of the accused (including his rights at the
court house and station house) are the Court's basic efforts to elaborate on certain provisions of the Bill of Rights. The Court is *not* attempting to protect the *criminal*. It is trying to protect the *innocent* from the
sometimes overwhelming physical and psychological pressures of the
police system. That criminals also take advantage of these protections

is inevitable; as long as the protections are accorded at all, they must be accorded to the guilty as well as the innocent.

Gideon v. *Wainwright* (1963) initiated the modern revolution in the rights of the accused. Gideon was accused of breaking and entering in Florida, a felony in that state. Unable to afford counsel, Gideon requested a court appointed lawyer and the judge responded:

> Mr. Gideon, I am sorry, but I cannot appoint Counsel to represent you in this case. Under the laws of the state of Florida, the only time the Court can appoint Counsel . . . is when that person is charged with a capital offense.

Gideon was convicted; after exhausting the Florida appeals procedures, he petitioned the Supreme Court for review.

Twenty-two states filed "friends of the court" briefs in the case urging that Gideon's request be made constitutionally demanding on all states. The American Civil Liberties Union also filed a brief arguing for Gideon.

Justice Hugo Black wrote the majority opinion. He declared that the right to counsel provision of the Sixth Amendment was "fundamental and essential to a fair trial." Florida was required to provide counsel to indigents.

The political developments prompted by the *Gideon* case and its offspring are recorded in the following section. Initially both federal and state governments, through their legislatures, instituted Public Defender systems or their equivalents. Through these systems the indigent in court was guaranteed the assistance of a trained and experienced lawyer to protect his rights.

Shortly after *Gideon*, the Supreme Court extended still further the demands of the Fifth and Sixth Amendments. In 1964 (*Escobedo* v. *Illinois*) the Court ruled that right to counsel must be granted *before* trial. Whenever the interrogation of a suspect moves from merely a general inquiry to accusation, the right to counsel comes into play. Further, any information obtained by the police in the absence of counsel during the accusatory stage is inadmissible in court. Where *Gideon* had been accepted by the states, Escobedo met strong opposition. In the case of *Miranda* v. *Arizona* (1966) the Court further limited the admissibility of confessions. To ensure that confessions which were used as evidence were voluntary, the police were required to warn a suspect of his right to remain silent and his right to counsel during interrogation. When the suspect waives these protections, the police must prove that the defendant understood the implications of the waiver.

Escobedo and Miranda immediately brought the Supreme Court under fire from Congress and the public. President Nixon's appointment of Warren Earl Burger, an advocate of "law and order" and "judicial restraint," to replace the retiring Earl Warren as Chief Justice was symptomatic of the pressures. The politics surrounding this series of cases illustrates well the political nature of the Supreme Court.

The impact of politics on Court decisions is also apparent. For example, it does appear the Court retreated under political pressures when it declared that Escobedo and Miranda would not apply retroactively. (Johnson v. New Jersey, 1965.) Convictions gained by means not in accord with the standards set by the two cases but which were gained prior to these cases were not to be reversed. Despite this concession Congress took steps to limit the Supreme Court's power to review the voluntariness of confessions in the Crime Control Act of 1968. Perhaps a further retrenchment or at least a holding action will occur as new cases come before the newly constituted Court under Chief Justice Warren Earl Burger. The following selection of readings records these and similar political responses to Court decisions concerning rights of the accused.

Right to Counsel and The 14th Amendment (1962)*

Gideon v. Wainwright

Prior to the Gideon decision, states were required to appoint counsel for the indigent in only two situations: (1) in capital cases involving a possible death penalty, and (2) in cases where "special circumstances"—such as illiteracy or mental illness—necessitated counsel. But Clarence Earl Gideon's handwritten petition to the Supreme Court helped widen the scope of right to counsel and began the revolution in criminal procedure. The majority opinion was written by Justice Black.

The Sixth Amendment provides, "In all criminal prosecutions, the accused shall enjoy the right . . . to have the Assistance of Counsel for his defense." We have construed this to mean that in federal courts counsel must be provided for defendants unable to employ counsel

---

*372 U.S. 335.

unless the right is competently and intelligently waived. [In *Betts* v. *Brady* it was] argued that this right is extended to indigent defendants in state courts by the Fourteenth Amendment. In response the Court stated that, while the Sixth Amendment laid down "no rule for the conduct laid by the Amendment upon the national courts expresses a rule so fundamental and essential to a fair trial, and so, to due process of law, that it is made obligatory upon the States by the Fourteenth Amendment." . . .

. . . .

We accept *Betts* v. *Brady's* assumption, based as it was on our prior cases, that a provision of the Bill of Rights which is "fundamental and essential to a fair trial" is made obligatory upon the States by the Fourteenth Amendment. We think the Court in *Betts* was wrong, however, in concluding that the Sixth Amendment's guarantee of counsel is not one of these fundamental rights.

. . . .

The fact is that in deciding as it did—that "appointment of counsel is not a fundamental right, essential to a fair trial"—the Court in *Betts* v. *Brady* made an abrupt break with its own well-considered precedents. In returning to these old precedents, sounder we believe than the new, we but restore constitutional principles established to achieve a fair system of justice. Not only these precedents but also reason and reflection require us to recognize that in our adversary system of criminal justice, any person haled into court, who is too poor to hire a lawyer, cannot be assured a fair trial unless counsel is provided for him. This seems to us to be an obvious truth. That government hires lawyers to prosecute and defendants who have the money hire lawyers to defend are the strongest indications of the widespread belief that lawyers in criminal courts are necessities, not luxuries. The right of one charged with crime to counsel may not be deemed fundamental and essential to fair trials in some countries, but it is in ours. From the very beginning, our state and national constitutions and laws have laid great emphasis on procedural and substantive safeguards designed to assure fair trials before impartial tribunals in which every defendant stands equal before the law. This noble ideal cannot be realized if the poor man charged with crime has to face his accusers without a lawyer to assist him. Florida, supported by two other states, has asked that *Betts* v. *Brady* be left intact. Twenty-two States, as friends of the Court, argue that *Betts* was "an anachronism when handed down" and that it should now be overruled. We agree.

. . . .

Gideon and Congress: The Criminal Justice Act of 1964*

Upon recommendation of President Kennedy, the Congress passed the Criminal Justice Act which assured adequate representation by counsel for the poor in federal courts. The following excerpts from the Senate Judiciary Committee's Report explain the Act.

To assure adequate representation in the Federal courts of accused persons with insufficient means, the Criminal Justice Act specifies a number of alternatives, or options, for assigning counsel; contemplates early appointment of counsel whose services are to continue throughout all stages of the proceedings: provides investigative, expert, and other services necessary to an adequate defense; and affords reasonable compensation to counsel who are assigned.

. . . .

Nearly 10,000 persons, more than 30 percent of the total number of defendants in Federal criminal cases, annually require court-appointed attorneys because they cannot afford to pay for their own. The inadequacy of the representation furnished by these lawyers is widely recognized. They are not paid for their services. They are not reimbursed for their out-of-pocket costs. They do not receive any investigative or expert help. They are not appointed until long after the arrest, when witnesses may have disappeared and leads grown stale. They often lack the trial experience essential for a competent defense. Taken together, these factors create a situation which falls far short of assuring equal justice to persons with insufficient means to provide for their own defense.

. . . .

This is the fourth successive Congress in which the committee has reported legislation to provide for the representation of defendants who are financially unable to obtain an adequate defense in criminal cases. Were we to need a reminder of how necessary such legislation is, none could be more emphatic than the Supreme Court's ruling in *Gideon* v. *Wainwright* this past term, which held that an accused who is unable to obtain counsel must be furnished one by the State. The Court stated that our Nation's concept of due process requires that poverty shall be no handicap in the defense of any person.

. . . .

Congressional Record, August 6, 1963, pp. S14221, 14223–4.

The opportunity to remedy our present, haphazard system is provided by S. 1057. Through the collective efforts of the Department of Justice, the Judicial Conference, the legal profession, and the Congress, the realization, not merely the aspiration, of "equal treatment for every litigant before the bar" can be achieved.

. . . .

The Shift From Investigation to Accusation Means Right to Counsel (1964)*

Escobedo v. *Illinois*

Using *Gideon* as precedent, the Justices of the Supreme Court extend right to counsel to the beginnings of the police process in the *Escobedo* case.

The Court majority argues that during the interrogation stage, when the case for the prosecution is largely developed, the accused must have support of counsel. The trial stage may be too late. Justice Goldberg delivered the opinion of the Court.

The critical question in this case is whether, under the circumstances, the refusal by the police to honor petitioner's request to consult with his lawyer during the course of an interrogation constitutes a denial of "the Assistance of Counsel" in violation of the Sixth Amendment to the Constitution as "made obligatory upon the States by the Fourteenth Amendment," (*Gideon* v. *Wainwright*). . . . and thereby renders inadmissible in a state criminal trial any incriminating statement elicited by the police during the interrogation. . . .

. . . .

The interrogation here was conducted before petitioner was formally indicted. But in the context of this case, that fact should make no difference. When petitioner requested, and was denied, an oppor-

---

*378 U.S. 478.

tunity to consult with his lawyer, the investigation had ceased to be a general investigation of "an unsolved crime." . . . Petitioner had become the accused, and the purpose of the interrogation was to "get him" to confess his guilt despite his constitutional right not to do so. At the time of his arrest and throughout the course of the interrogation, the police told petitioner that they had convincing evidence that he had fired the fatal shots. Without informing him of his absolute right to remain silent in the face of this accusation, the police urged him to make a statement. . . . Petitioner, a layman, was undoubtedly unaware that under Illinois law an admission of "mere" complicity in the murder plot was legally as damaging as an admission of firing of the fatal shots. . . . The "guiding hand of counsel" was essential to advise petitioner of his rights in this delicate situation. . . . This was the "stage when legal aid and advice" were most critical to petitioner. . . . What happened at this interrogation could certainly "affect the whole trial," . . . since rights "may be as irretrievably lost, if not then and there asserted, as they are when an accused represented by counsel waives a right for strategic purposes." . . . It would exalt form over substance to make the right to counsel, under these circumstances, depend on whether at the time of the interrogation, the authorities had secured a formal indictment. Petitioner had, for all practical purposes, already been charged with murder. . . .

In *Gideon* v. *Wainwright* we held that every person accused of a crime, whether state or federal, is entitled to a lawyer at trial. The rule sought by the State here, however, would make the trial no more than an appeal from the interrogation; and the "right to use counsel at the formal trial [would be] a very hollow thing [if], for all practical purposes, the conviction is already assured by pretrial examination." . . .

It is argued that if the right to counsel is afforded prior to indictment, the number of confessions obtained by the police will diminish significantly, because most confessions are obtained during the period between arrest and indictment, and "any lawyer worth his salt will tell the suspect in no uncertain terms to make no statement to police under any circumstances." . . . This argument, of course, cuts two ways. The fact that many confessions are obtained during this period points up its critical nature as a "stage when legal aid and advice" are surely needed. . . .

. . . .

We hold, therefore, that where, as here, the investigation is no longer a general inquiry into an unsolved crime but has begun to focus on a particular suspect, the suspect has been taken into police custody, the police carry out a process of interrogations that lends itself to eliciting incriminating statements, the suspect has requested and been denied an opportunity to consult with his lawyer, and the police have not effectively warned him of his absolute constitutional right to remain silent, the accused has been denied "the Assistance of Counsel" in violation of the Sixth Amendment to the Constitution as "made obligatory upon the States by the Fourteenth Amendment" (*Gideon* v. *Wainwright*), . . . and that no statement elicited by the police during the interrogation may be used against him at a criminal trial. . . . We hold only that when the process shifts from investigatory to accusatory—when its focus is on the accused and its purpose is to elicit a confession—our adversary system begins to operate, and, under the circumstances here, the accused must be permitted to consult with his lawyer.

·   ·   ·   ·   ·   ·   ·   ·   ·   ·   ·   ·   ·   ·   ·   ·   ·   ·

Justice Byron White, wrote a dissenting opinion.

The Court holds that once the accused becomes a suspect and, presumably, is arrested, any admission made to the police thereafter is inadmissible in evidence unless the accused has waived his right to counsel. The decision is thus another major step in the direction of the goal which the Court seemingly has in mind—to bar from evidence all admissions obtained from an individual suspected of crime, whether involuntarily made or not. . . .

The right to counsel now not only entitles the accused to counsel's advice and aid in preparing for trial but stands as an impenetrable barrier to any interrogation once the accused has become a suspect.

·   ·   ·   ·   ·   ·   ·   ·   ·   ·   ·   ·   ·   ·   ·   ·   ·   ·

This new American judge's rule, which is to be applied in both federal and state courts, is perhaps thought to be a necessary safeguard against the possibility of extorted confessions. To this extent it reflects a deepseated distrust of law enforcement officers everywhere, unsupported by relevant data or current material based upon our own experience. Obviously law enforcement officers can make mistakes and exceed their authority, as today's decision shows that even judges can do, but I have somewhat more faith than the Court evidently has in the ability and desire of prosecutors and of the power of the appellate courts to discern and correct such violations of the law.

·   ·   ·   ·   ·   ·   ·   ·   ·   ·   ·   ·   ·   ·   ·   ·   ·   ·

The States and Right to Counsel (1965)*

The following reading illustrates the response of States to the demands of the *Gideon* ruling. Although most States had already provided means by which the poor could obtain counsel in some cases, the Public Defender system appears to allow for well trained and specialized lawyers at the local level to handle the increase in cases involving the indigent.

Ordinance No. 244:

Section 3

1. When a defendant is brought before Magistrate upon an arrest, either with or without warrant, on a charge of having committed a public offense, the Magistrate shall immediately inform him of the charge against him and of his right to the aid of legal counsel at every stage of the proceedings and before any further proceedings are had.

2. Any defendant charged with a felony or a gross misdemeanor who is an indigent may, by written application addressed to the District Court and delivered to the Magistrate, request the appointment of legal counsel to represent him.

.   .   .   .

Section 5

1. The Public Defender, when designated by the appropriate Judge of [State] District Court pursuant to the provisions of this ordinance, shall represent, without charge, each indigent person who is under arrest and held for a crime which constitutes a felony or gross misdemeanor, or in any other proper case when appointed by the Court.

2. When so representing an indigent person the Public Defender shall:

(a) counsel and defend him, if he is held in custody and charged with a public offense amounting to a felony or gross misdemeanor, or in insanity or incompetency proceedings or in

---

*The State of Nevada enacted enabling legislation in 1965 (Assembly Bill #199, NRS Chap. 279) and Clark County (Nevada), through funding assistance from the Ford Foundation, instituted the Public Defender System in Ordinance No. 244.

　　　　any other proper case, at every stage of the proceedings follow-
　　　　ing such designation by the appropriate Judge of the District
　　　　Court.

　(b)　prosecute any appeals or other remedies before or after con-
　　　　viction or commitment that he considers to be in the interests
　　　　of justice.

Confessions and The Fifth Amendment (1966)*

Miranda v. *Arizona*

In the following set of cases the Supreme Court changed its emphasis from the right to counsel as a protection for the accused to the
right to remain silent. The voluntariness of confessions was the specific
issue. Unless the accused is fully informed of his rights and the implications of waiving these rights, any confession is inadmissible in court.
Thus, the Fifth Amendment provides the Court with a Constitutional
basis for its decisions. The opinion is by Chief Justice Warren.

The cases before us raise questions which go to the roots of our
concepts of American criminal jurisprudence: the restraints society
must observe consistent with the federal Constitution in prosecuting
individuals for crime. More specifically, we deal with the admissibility
of statements obtained from an individual who is subjected to custodial police interrogation and the necessity for procedures which
assure that the individual is accorded his privilege under the Fifth
Amendment to the Constitution not to be compelled to incriminate
himself.

· · · · · · · · · · · · · · · · · ·

We have undertaken a thorough re-examination of the *Escobedo*
decision and the principles it announced, and we reaffirm it. That
case was but an explication of basic rights that are enshrined in our
Constitution—that "No person . . . shall be compelled in any criminal
case to be a witness against himself," and that "the accused shall . . .

---

*384 U.S. 436.

have the Assistance of Counsel"—rights which were put in jeopardy in that case through official overbearing.

. . . .

An understanding of the nature and setting of in-custody interrogation is essential to our decisions today. The difficulty in depicting what transpires at such interrogations stems from the fact that in this country they have largely taken place incommunicado. From extensive factual studies undertaken in the early 1930s, including the famous Wickersham Report to Congress by a Presidential Commission, it is clear that police violence and the "third degree" flourished at that time. The 1961 Commission on Civil Rights found much evidence to indicate that "some policemen still resort to physical force to obtain confessions." . . . The use of physical brutality and violence is not, unfortunately, relegated to the past or to any part of the country. . . .

. . . .

[T]he modern practice of in-custody interrogation is psychologically rather than physically oriented. As we have stated before, ... this Court has recognized that coercion can be mental as well as physical, and that the blood of the accused is not the only hallmark of an unconstitutional inquisition. . . . Interrogation still takes place in privacy. . . .

To be alone with the subject is essential to prevent distraction and to deprive him of any outside support. The aura of confidence in his guilt undermines his will to resist. He merely confirms the preconceived story the police seem to have him describe. Patience and persistence, at times relentless questioning, are employed. To obtain a confession, the interrogator must "patiently maneuver himself or his quarry into a position from which the desired object may be obtained." When normal procedures fail to produce the needed result, the police may resort to deceptive stratagems such as giving false legal advice. It is important to keep the subject off balance, for example, by trading on his insecurity about himself or his surroundings. The police then persuade, trick, or cajole him out of exercising his constitutional rights.

. . . .

In these cases, we might not find the defendants' statements to have been involuntary in traditional terms. Our concern for adequate safeguards to protect precious Fifth Amendment rights is, of course, not lessened in the slightest. In each of the cases, the defendant was thrust into an unfamiliar atmosphere and run through menacing police interrogation procedures. . . . [T]he records do not evince overt physical coercion or patented psychological ploys. The fact remains that in none of these cases did the officers undertake to afford appropriate safeguards at the outset of the interrogation to insure that the statements were truly the product of free choice. . . . This atmosphere carries its own badge of intimidation. To be sure, this is not physical intimidation, but it is equally destructive of human dignity. The current practice of incommunicado interrogation is at odds with one of our Nation's most cherished principles—that the individual may not be compelled to incriminate himself. Unless adequate protective devices are employed to dispel the compulsion inherent in custodial surroundings, no statement obtained from the defendant can truly be the product of his free choice.

. . . .

At the outset, if a person in custody is to be subjected to interrogation, he must first be informed in clear and unequivocal terms that he has the right to remain silent. . . .

. . . .

The warning of the right to remain silent must be accompanied by the explanation that anything said can and will be used against the individual in court. This warning is needed in order to make him aware not only of the privilege, but also of the consequences of forgoing it. . . . [T]his warning may serve to make the individual more acutely aware that he is faced with a phase of the adversary system— that he is not in the presence of persons acting solely in his interest.

The circumstances surrounding in-custody interrogation can operate very quickly to overbear the will of one merely made aware of his privilege by his interrogators. Therefore, the right to have counsel present at the interrogation is indispensable to the protection of the Fifth Amendment privilege under the system we delineate today. Our aim is to assure that the individual's right to choose between silence and speech remains unfettered throughout the interrogation process. Thus, the need for counsel to protect the Fifth Amendment privilege comprehends not merely a right to consult with counsel prior to questioning, but also to have counsel present during any questioning if the defendant so desires.

. . . .

An individual need not make a pre-interrogation request for a lawyer. While such request affirmatively secures his right to have one, his failure to ask for a lawyer does not constitute a waiver. The accused who does not know his rights and therefore does not make a request may be the person who most needs counsel.

.   .   .   .

The financial ability of the individual has no relationship to the scope of the rights involved here. The privilege against self-incrimination secured by the Constitution applies to all individuals. The need for counsel in order to protect the privilege exists for the indigent as well as the affluent. . . .

.   .   .   .

To summarize, we hold that when an individual is taken into custody or otherwise deprived of his freedom by the authorities and is subjected to questioning, the privilege against self-incrimination is jeopardized. He must be warned prior to any questioning that he has the right to remain silent, that anything he says can be used against him in a court of law, that he has the right to the presence of an attorney, and that if he cannot afford an attorney one will be appointed for him prior to any questioning if he so desires. Opportunity to exercise these rights must be afforded to him throughout the interrogation. After such warnings have been given and such opportunity afforded him, the individual may knowingly and intelligently waive these rights and agree to answer questions or make a statement. But unless and until such warnings and waiver are demonstrated by the prosecution at trial, no evidence obtained as a result of interrogation can be used against him. . . .

In announcing these principles, we are not unmindful of the burdens which law enforcement officials must bear, often under trying circumstances. We also fully recognize the obligation of all citizens to aid in enforcing the criminal laws. This Court, while protecting individual rights, has always given ample latitude to law enforcement agencies in the legitimate exercise of their duties. The limits we have placed on the interrogation process should not constitute an undue interference with a proper system of law enforcement. . . .

Justice John Harlan, joined by Justice Potter Stewart and Justice Byron White, dissented.

I believe the decision of the Court represents poor constitutional law and entails harmful consequences for the country at large.

.   .   .   .

The new rules are not designed to guard against police brutality or other unmistakably banned forms of coercion. Those who use third-degree tactics and deny them in court are equally able and destined to lie as skillfully about warnings and waivers. Rather, the thrust of the new rules is to negate all pressures, to reinforce the nervous or ignorant suspect, and ultimately to discourage any confession at all. The aim in short is toward "voluntariness" in a utopian sense, or to view it from a different angle, voluntariness with a vengeance.

To incorporate this notion into the Constitution requires a strained reading of history and precedent and a disregard of the very pragmatic concerns that alone may on occasion justify such strains.

. . . .

[T]he Court is taking a real risk with society's welfare in imposing its new regime on the country. The social costs of crime are too great to call the new rules anything but a hazardous experimentation.

. . . .

The Lower Courts and *Miranda* (1967)*
"Confessed Killer of Six Goes Free"

A man who admitted slaying his wife and five small children walked out of a Brooklyn courtroom yesterday, free, because the only available evidence against him was his own confession.

The defendant, Jose Suarez, 22 years, a factory worker, was arrested on April 27, 1966. Questioned by the police, he signed a statement, acknowledging having killed his common-law wife, Maria Torres, 24; their children, Yvette, 4; Nancy, 3; and Jose, 11 months, also Harry Santiago, 5, and Maria Antonio, 2.

Suarez said in the confession that after his wife had cut his leg with a knife during an argument, he seized the weapon and stabbed her and the children more than 100 times. That was on April 23 in their home at 301 Hooper Street.

On June 13 the United States Supreme Court ruled in the landmark *Miranda* case that a defendant in custody must be informed of his rights. These include the right to remain silent if he wishes to, the

---

*© 1967–1969 by the New York Times Company. Reprinted with permission from *New York Times*, February 21, 1967, p. 41.

right to consult a lawyer and the right to a warning that anything he says may be used against him at trial.

Suarez was advised on none of these points, since New York State law at the time did not require it. However, the *Miranda* decision applied to him, inasmuch as it was made retroactive to cover all defendants who had not yet been tried.

Last month, three men were freed in murder trials here by State Supreme Court justices after rulings that they had not been informed of their right to counsel before they confessed.

. . . .

For seven months the office of District Attorney Aaron A. Koota and the police sought, without success, to obtain evidence other than the confession against Suarez. A grand jury finally indicted him on Nov. 4. One week later, with a lawyer, Suarez retracted the confession and pleaded not guilty.

"I daresay that if his questioning had conformed with the requirements of *Miranda*, this defendant would be in Sing Sing Prison serving several life sentences," Assistant District Attorney Nathan R. Schor told the court yesterday, "I am now constrained to ask for dismissal of the indictment."

. . . .

State Supreme Court Justice Michael Kern then spoke.

"Unfortunately the general public doesn't understand the law. Even an animal such as this one, and I believe this is insulting the animal kingdom, must be protected with all the legal safeguards.

"This is a very sad thing. It is so repulsive it makes one's blood run cold and any decent human being's stomach turn to let a thing like this out on the street."

Leaning forward, Justice Kern addressed the prosecutor. "Are you sure, I ask you most seriously, whether his (confession) is all you have in this case?"

Mr. Schor replied: "I say reluctantly, with a heavy heart, that we simply have no alternative. There is no other evidence."

. . . .

Last night Mr. Koota issued the following statement:

"The United States Supreme Court has weighted the scales of justice heavily in favor of the criminal suspect. I am not a prophet, but the handwriting on the wall indicates a trend on the part of the Court to outlaw all confessions made to police. If and when the melancholy day comes, the death knell of effective criminal law enforcement will have been sounded."

The Challenge of Crime in a Free Society:
A Dissenting View (1967)*

Seven members of the President's Commission on Law Enforcement and the Administration of Justice issued a minority report accusing the twelve-member majority of not dealing directly with the problems created by the Supreme Court decisions in *Escobedo* and *Miranda* and making separate recommendations for handling those problems. The Commission's Report had limited its recommendations on *Gideon* and *Miranda* exclusively to means by which right to counsel should be implemented.

The strong emotions engendered by [Supreme Court] decisions, for and against both them and the Court, have inhibited rational discourse as to their actual effect upon law enforcement. There has been unfair—and even destructive—criticism of the Court itself. Many have failed to draw the line, fundamental in a democratic society, between the right to discuss and analyze the effect of particular decisions, and the duty to support and defend the judiciary, and particularly the Supreme Court, as an institution essential to freedom.

Whatever the reason, the trend of decisions strikingly has been towards strengthening the rights of accused persons and limiting the powers of law enforcement. It is a trend which has accelerated rapidly at a time when the nation is deeply concerned with its apparent inability to deal successfully with the problem of crime.

.   .   .   .

The broadened rights and resulting restraints upon law enforcement which have had the greatest impact are those derived from the Fifth Amendment privilege against self-incrimination and the Sixth Amendment assurance of counsel.

The two cases which have caused the greatest concern are *Escobedo* v. *Illinois* and *Miranda* v. *Arizona.* . . .

.   .   .   .

If the majority opinion in *Miranda* is implemented in its full sweep, it could mean the virtual elimination of pretrial interrogation of suspects—on the street, at the scene of a crime, and in the station

---

*Reprinted from the minority report of the President's Commission on Law Enforcement and Administration of Justice, *The Challenge of Crime in a Free Society* (U.S.: Government Printing Office, 1967), pp. 304–308.

house—because there would then be no such interrogation without the presence of counsel unless the person detained, howsoever briefly, waives this right.

.   .   .   .

The impact of *Miranda* on the use of confessions is an equally serious problem. Indeed, this is the other side of the coin. If interrogations are muted there will be no confessions; if they are tainted, resulting confessions—as well as other related evidence—will be excluded or the convictions subsequently set aside. There is real reason for the concern, expressed by dissenting justices, that *Miranda* in effect proscribes the use of all confessions. This would be the most far-reaching departure from precedent and established practice in the history of our criminal law.

.   .   .   .

The question which we raise is whether, even with the support of a deeply concerned President and the implementation of the Commission's national strategy against crime, law enforcement can effectively discharge its vital role in "controlling crime and violence" without changes in existing constitutional limitations.

There is no more sacred part of our history or our constitutional structure than the Bill of Rights. One approaches the thought of the most limited amendment with reticence and a full awareness both of the political obstacles and the inherent delicacy of drafting changes which preserve all relevant values. But it must be remembered that the Constitution contemplates amendment, and no part of it should be so sacred that it remains beyond review.

Whatever can be done to right the present imbalance through legislation or rule of court should have high priority. The promising criminal justice programs of the American Bar Association and the American Law Institute should be helpful in this respect. But reform and clarification will fall short unless they achieve these ends:

An adequate opportunity must be provided the police for interrogation at the scene of the crime, during investigations and at the station house, with appropriate safeguards to prevent abuse.

The legitimate place of voluntary confessions in law enforcement must be reestablished and their use made dependent upon meeting due process standards of voluntariness.

Provision must be made for comment on the failure of an accused to take the stand, and also for reciprocal discovery in criminal cases.

If, as now appears likely, a constitutional amendment is required to strengthen law enforcement in these respects, the American people should face up to the need and undertake necessary action without delay.

. . . .

Congress and *Miranda* (1968)*
Debates on Omnibus Crime Control and Safe Streets Act of 1967

Congress led the attack on the Court's decisions in *Escobedo* and *Miranda*. The proposed Crime Control Act of 1967 was the vehicle by which the legislators recorded their displeasure with the high court rulings. The remarks of Senator John McClellan (D., Ark.) are typical. Speaking in defense of the Court was another group of Congressmen— represented by Senator Joseph Tydings (D., Md.). The critics did succeed, via Title II of the Act, in leaving to the trial court judge the determination of the admissibility of confessions. Thus, lower courts would establish the voluntariness of confessions.

SENATOR McCLELLAN: Mr. President,
When I addressed the Senate last Friday, May 17, I said:

> The true issue, and there is no escaping it, is the spiraling rate of crime and the erroneous decisions of the Supreme Court versus the safety of our people and the security of our country.

Mr. President, as to the Constitution, I have just as much reverence for it as any Member of this body. What I deplore is Supreme Court Justices, who are sworn to it, as it has been upheld all down through the history of our Republic, themselves joining in opinions that say it means one thing, and then, when the next case comes along, turning a complete somersault in order to amend the Constitution.
Respect? Where? It is not with five members of the Supreme Court.

. . . .

Congressional Record, May 21, 1968, pp. S 6009–S 6012.

Let us look at the reality of the moment. I ask Senators to look at the two charts which have been placed here in the Chamber—one depicting "crime clocks," and the other one showing the relative rise of crime and population, percentagewise, from 1944 through 1967.

These charts show that since the *Miranda* decision, crime has increased 137½ per cent. Tell me it had no impact. Look at the *Mallory* case. Look at the *Escobedo* case. Look at the *Miranda* case. The graph is still turning in a spiral upward and upward, Mr. President.

It will be noted that the crime clock shows that there are six serious crimes committed each minute; a murder is committed every 48 minutes; a forcible rape every 21 minutes; aggravated assault every 2 minutes; one robbery every 3½ minutes; one burglary every 23 seconds; one larceny every 35 seconds; and one auto theft every 57 seconds.

Can we, Members of the U.S. Senate, in good conscience, . . . fiddle, procrastinate, and wait for an indefinite study with crime so rampant in our land as it is today?

I do not think so. Are we going to fiddle while crime destroys America, or are we going to stand up, like men, and vote to do something about it? We can excuse and alibi until doomsday, but all the time we are doing it, crime is increasing.

Will we in this hour of decision and opportunity fail to measure up while the crime rate is rising now at a rate of fifteen to twenty per cent each year—eight to ten times faster than the increase in population?

.   .   .   .

Who wants this confessions provision in Title II defeated? The answer is, primarily those who will benefit from it most. Who are they? If this confessions provision is defeated, the lawbreaker will be further encouraged and reassured that he can continue a life of crime and depredations profitably with impunity and without punishment. If it is defeated, the protection of society and the safety of good people —of the innocent throughout the land, your constituents and mine— will be placed in everincreasing peril as the crime rate continues to spiral onward and upward to intolerable heights of danger.

.   .   .   .

If this effort to deal with these erroneous Court decisions is defeated, every gangster and overlord of the underworld; every syndicate chief, racketeer, captain, lieutenant, sergeant, private, punk, and hoodlum in organized crime; every murderer, rapist, robber, burglar, arsonist, thief, and con-man will have cause to rejoice and celebrate.

Whereas, if it is defeated, the safety of decent people will be placed in greater jeopardy and every innocent, law-abiding, and God-fearing citizen in this land will have cause to weep and despair.

SENATOR TYDINGS: Mr. President, I served for three years as the principal prosecutor of the District of Maryland. I personally have not agreed with all the decisions which have been handed down by the High Court. But I should like to set the record straight on a few points.

The *Miranda* decision basically says that when a defendant is arrested, the arresting officer should tell that individual that he has the right to remain silent, that anything he says can be held against him, that he has a right to consult a lawyer, and if he is too poor, the court will appoint one.

I challenge the statements of the Senator from Arkansas when he says that organized crime and the hoodlums it employs will benefit from these simple rules of procedure. Mr. President, that simply is not factual. There is no professional criminal today who, when he is arrested, does not automatically realize his rights and call up his attorney. No son of a rich man, no young man who has had the benefit of a college education, none of our children or our friends' children, need these protections generally.

They already know their rights and privileges. However, when we take away the rights and privileges of the weakest and the most defenseless and the most innocent, we are taking away the rights of the whole Nation.

The rules of procedure in *Miranda* have not, in my judgment and in the judgment of each comprehensive survey made of the facts afterwards—and not based on pure speculation and passion—these rules have not affected law enforcement in the rate of convictions, the rate of arrests, or the rate of clearance of criminal cases.

.   .   .   .

The reason for the rule against self-incrimination and the granting of the privilege against self-incrimination is to protect the innocent.

.   .   .   .

The proponents of Title II say that the *Miranda* case went further. Those who attacked the decision of the Supreme Court in *Brown* v. *Mississippi* said: "Why, the Supreme Court has never before reviewed the voluntariness of a confession which has been passed on by the highest court of a sovereign State."

Certainly they broke new ground. However, it was done to protect the rights of the innocent. It was to vindicate the basic privilege against self-incrimination, which is the foundation of any democratic society.

.   .   .   .

I have indicated that I do not defend all of the decisions of the Supreme Court. There are decisions in which, if I had been on the Court, I would have been in dissent myself. However, our system is based on a delicate balance of power, and the Supreme Court is the top of our judicial system.

Mr. President, this is the way the drafters of our Constitution wanted it. This is the way our Republic has worked. Attacks on the Supreme Court, which is the basis of Title II, are not unusual in the history of this country. . . .

. . . .

Mr. President, the issue before the Senate is whether or not we are going to take a step backward in those rights and individual liberties as interpreted by the Supreme Court of the United States which our Bill of Rights and our Constitution provide for every American, whether they are rich or poor, and whether they are weak or strong.

. . . .

I oppose Title II for two reasons. First, it is an attack on our delicate constitutional system. Make no mistake about it, it is an attack on the Federal judiciary and the Supreme Court. It endangers the system of checks and balances we have in this country. Second, I oppose it because, in my judgment, it will cause massive confusion in all law-enforcement offices throughout the States.

Crime Control Act of 1968*

Title II

Sec. 701.

(a) Chapter 223, title 18, United States Code (relating to witnesses and evidence), is amended by adding at the end thereof the following new sections:

3501. Admissibility of Confessions

a. In any criminal prosecution brought by the United States or by the District of Columbia, a confession, as defined in subsection

---

*Reprinted from Public Law 90-351 (1968).

(e) hereof, shall be admissible in evidence if it is voluntarily given. Before such confession is received in evidence, the trial judge shall, out of the presence of the jury, determine any issue as to voluntariness. If the trial judge determines that the confession was voluntarily made it shall be admitted in evidence and the trial judge shall permit the jury to hear relevant evidence on the issue of voluntariness and shall instruct the jury to give such weight to the confession as the jury feels it deserves under all the circumstances.

b. The trial judge in determining the issue of voluntariness shall take into consideration all the circumstances surrounding the giving of the confession, including (1) the time elapsing between arrest and arraignment of the defendant making the confession, if it was made after arrest and before arraignment, (2) whether such defendant knew the nature of the offense with which he was charged or of which he was suspected at the time of making the confession, (3) whether or not such defendant was advised or knew that he was not required to make any statement and that any such statement could be used against him, (4) whether or not such defendant had been advised prior to questioning of his right to the assistance of counsel, and (5) whether or not such defendant was without the assistance of counsel when questioned and when giving such confession.

The presence or absence of any of the above-mentioned factors to be taken into consideration by the judge need not be conclusive on the issue of voluntariness of the confession.

c. In any criminal prosecution by the United States or by the District of Columbia, a confession made or given by a person who is a defendant therein, while such person was under arrest or other detention in the custody of any law-enforcement officer or law-enforcement agency, shall not be inadmissible solely because of delay in bringing such person before a commissioner or other officer empowered to commit persons charged with offenses against the laws of the United States or of the District of Columbia if such confession is found by the trial judge to have been made voluntarily and if the weight to be given the confession is left to the jury and if such confession was made or given by such person within six hours immediately following his arrest or other detention: . . . .

d. Nothing contained in this section shall bar the admission in evidence of any confession made or given voluntarily by any person to any other person without interrogation by anyone, or at any time at which the person who made or gave such confession was not under arrest or other detention.

e. As used in this section, the term "confession" means any confession of guilt of any criminal offense or any self-incriminating statement made or given orally or in writing.

Amend The Fifth Amendment (1968)*

Judge Henry J. Friendly

One proposed solution to the restrictions imposed on prosecutors and police by the Supreme Court rulings on the rights of the accused is to amend the Fifth Amendment to allow greater scope to what is admissible in trials. Judge Friendly suggests such an amendment which would "correct" the *Miranda* standards.

Henry J. Friendly, a Federal appellate judge who has been mentioned as a possible Nixon appointee to the Supreme Court, has proposed a constitutional amendment to reverse a number of liberal Supreme Court decisions on criminal law.

The Supreme Court, he said, has expanded the Fifth Amendment's privilege against self-incrimination far beyond its intended scope, to the point that it "seriously impeded the state in the most basic of all tasks, to provide for the security of the individual and his property."

"The time has come," Judge Friendly said, "when the nation should face up to the hard task of considering an amendment to the self-incrimination clause that will preserve all the framers said and some of the Court's extensions, modify others, expunge some altogether and guard against accretions quite obviously in the making."

. . . .

Judge Friendly asserted that the Supreme Court had tended to read . . . [the Fifth Amendment] as protecting defendants from cooperating with the police, before or during a trial.

In this vein, he criticized *Miranda* v. *Arizona*, a decision handed down in 1966. It gives suspects a Fifth-Amendment right not to be questioned outside the presence of counsel.

. . . .

*© 1968–1969 by the New York Times Company. Reprinted with permission from *New York Times*, November 10, 1968, p. 73, Henry J. Friendly, and the *Cincinnati Law Review*.

Judge Friendly said that unless the Court's membership changed drastically it might soon restrict the state's authority to use a suspect's hair, blood, handwriting, voice or other personal elements without his consent.

He proposed a 350-word amendment to the Constitution that would specify that the self-incrimination clause shall not be construed to prohibit:

. . . .

1. Interrogating any person or requesting him to furnish goods or chattels, including books, papers and other writings, without warning that he is not obliged to comply, unless such person has been taken into custody because of, or has been charged with, a crime to which the interrogation or request relates.

2. Comment by the judge at any criminal trial on previous refusal by the defendant to answer relevant inquiries before a grand jury or similar investigating body, or before a judicial officer charged with the duty of presiding over his interrogation, provided that he shall have had the assistance of counsel when being so questioned and shall have then been warned that he need not answer; that if he does answer, his answer may be used against him in court; and that if he does not answer, the judge may comment on his refusal.

3. Compulsory production, in response to reasonable sub-poena or similar process, of any good or chattels, including books, papers and other writings.

4. Dismissal, suspension or other discipline of any officer or employee of the United States, a state or any agency or subdivision thereof, or any person licensed by any of them, for refusal, after warning of the consequences, to answer a relevant question concerning his official or professional conduct in any investigation relating thereto, or the introduction in evidence of any answer given to any such question, provided that such person shall have had the assistance of counsel.

5. Requiring a person lawfully arrested for or charged with crime to identify himself and make himself available for visual and auditory investigation and for reasonable scientific and medical tests, provided the assistance of counsel has been furnished except when urgency otherwise requires.

6. Requiring registration or reporting reasonably necessary for a proper governmental purpose, provided no registration or report so compelled shall be admissible as evidence of any crime revealed therein.

Chief Justice Burger and the Constitution (1969)*

The appointment as Chief Justice of Warren Earl Burger was hailed by many as a harbinger of a new era. By appointing a "strict constructionist," President Nixon appeared to be supporting the critics of the Court. While serving on the U.S. Court of Appeals Burger delivered two speeches which illustrate the thinking regarding the role of the Supreme Court he will take with him to the court of last resort.

Columbus Speech

Too many law professors for a long time gave uncritical applause to anything and everything they could identify as an expansion of individual "rights," even when that expansion was at the expense of the rights of other human beings—the innocent citizens—presumably protected by the same Constitution. I see signs of a constructively critical attitude by law teachers toward some of the judicial techniques employed in recent years to make reforms in criminal law procedure and rules of evidence.

As we look back we can see that for about the first 150 years of our history the criminal law and its procedures remained fairly simple and quite stable. For 25 to 30 years after that there was a considerable ferment in criminal procedure and the rules of evidence, and in the last 10 years, more or less, we have witnessed what many scholars describe as a "revolution in criminal law."

Today we have the most complicated system of criminal justice and the most difficult system to administer of any country in the world. To a large extent this is a result of judicial decisions which in effect made drastic revisions of the code of criminal procedure and evidence, and to a substantial extent imposed these procedures on the states.

This was indeed a revolution and some of these changes made were long overdue. All lawyers take pride, for example, in a case like *Gideon* v. *Wainwright*, which guarantees a lawyer to every person charged with a serious offense. The holdings of the Supreme Court on right to counsel, on trial by jury instead of trial by press, and on coerced confession will always stand out as landmarks on basic rights.

---

*Excerpts from speeches by the new Chief Justice delivered at Columbus, Ohio (Sept. 4, 1968) and Ripon College (March 14, 1969) while he was still on the bench of the U.S. Court of Appeals. *New York Times*, May 22, 1969, p. 37.

These were appropriate subjects for definitive constitutional holdings rather than for rulemaking procedure to which I now turn. (In fairness, it must be said that some states had achieved these improvements long before the Supreme Court did so.)

My central point tonight is, that as we look back, it seems clear now that the Supreme Court should have used the mechanism provided by Congress for making rules of criminal procedure rather than changing the criminal procedure and rules of evidence on a case-by-case basis.

.   .   .   .

I suggest to you that a large measure of responsibility for some of the bitterness in American life today over the administration of criminal justice can fairly be laid to the method which the Supreme Court elected to use for this comprehensive—this enormous—task. My thesis assumes the correctness of the objectives the Court sought to reach in all of these controversial holdings. To put this in simple terms, the Supreme Court helped make the problems we now have because it did not "go by the book" and use the tested, although admittedly slow, process of rulemaking through use of the advisory committee mechanism provided by Congress 30 years ago.

I question tonight not the Court or the last decade's holdings of the Court but its methodology and the loose ends, confusion and bitterness that methodology has left in its wake. There is no legitimate place in American life for some of the acrimonious, irrational criticism of the Supreme Court and it ought to stop.

Ripon Speech

We often hear the claim that the breakdown of law and order is due to this decision or that decision of some court—most often of the Supreme Court.

It would be good if things were that simple, for, if the overruling of one or two opinions would solve the problems of crime, I suspect the Supreme Court would be willing to reconsider.

It is no aid to sensible public discourse to attribute the crime problem to any one decision or any court.

The celebrated case which takes five to ten years to complete is common talk in the best clubs and the worst ghettos. If lax police work and lax prosecution will impair the deterrent effects of the law, repeated reversals and multiple trials in the highly publicized cases will likely have a similar effect.

Is a society which frequently takes five to ten years to dispose of a single criminal case entitled to call itself an "organized" society? Is a judicial system, which consistently finds it necessary to try a criminal case three, four or five times deserving of the confidence and respect of decent people?

In part the terrible price we are paying in crime is because we have tended—once the drama of the trial is over—to regard all criminals as human rubbish.

Is the Court Handcuffing the Cops? (1969)*

James Vorenberg and James Q. Wilson

Professors Vorenberg and Wilson of Harvard University point out that the effect of the Supreme Court's decision on crime is minimal. Thus, curbing the Court will have very little impact on crime prevention. Americans, they argue, must reject simplistic solutions and reappraise their entire approach to the control of crime. Legislators, executives, the courts and the public must be concerned with the basic causes of crime rather than with dealing with the accused after a crime has been committed.

Vorenberg

In my view, the contest between the police and the United States Supreme Court is grossly exaggerated. In any event, that contest, to the extent that it exists at all, has very little to do with crime. What the Supreme Court does has practically no effect on the amount of crime in this country, and what the police do has far less effect than is generally believed. The nation seems to have its attention riveted on a largely irrelevant, over-dramatized confrontation between the police and the Court, and thus is impeded in doing anything constructive about crime—or even understanding it.

New York Times Magazine (May 11, 1969), VI, p. 32. © 1969 by The New York Times Company. Reprinted with permission of the *New York Times*, James Vorenberg, and James Q. Wilson. This article was adapted from a recording of a forum sponsored by the Harvard Club of N.Y.C. and the Associated Harvard Alumni at Town Hall, N.Y.

The controversy over confessions is probably the best example of how the effect of Supreme Court decisions on the volume of crime has been exaggerated. The principal target of those who attack the Court is the *Miranda* decision of 1966. . . .

What is suggested is that this decision is in some way accountable for a very large rise in crime that has occurred since 1966. But what are the facts? In the first place, the President's Commission on Law Enforcement and Administration of Justice, which is generally known as the Crime Commission, found that only something between one-tenth and one-third of the crimes committed are even reported to the police.

It's not very likely that a decision that deals only with people in custody is going to have much effect on crimes that are not even reported to the police.

We also found in one study that, of those crimes that are reported to the police, only one-quarter lead to arrest. And of those that do lead to arrest, only a small proportion are cases where a confession is crucial to solution. The others are cases where there is a witness or some piece of tangible evidence.

Already we are probably down to a maximum of one per cent or two per cent for cases in which *Miranda* could have a direct impact. Then we have to take account of the fact that, in many cases since *Miranda*, the suspect still confesses, and that, in many cases before *Miranda*, the suspect did not confess. The result is that the maximum direct statistical impact of this much-reviled decision is of the order of a fraction of one per cent.

But, it is said, there is more to it than that: *Miranda* in some way provides general encouragement to potential criminals. What that means is that, to get the encouragement *Miranda* is said to provide, before I set out to commit a crime I have to go through the following reasoning process: "If I commit this crime, and if I'm caught, and if I confess, that confession can be excluded if the police don't offer me counsel." I suggest that, in view of what little we do know about people who are committing crimes, and the conditions under which those crimes take place, it is unlikely that that rather elaborate hypothetical reasoning process is going on.

Then it is said by the critics of *Miranda*: "It's not what *Miranda* actually says that has such a demoralizing effect on the police and encourages crime. It's what it is thought to mean, what the exaggerated view of it is." An obvious first step to remedying this effect of *Miranda* is for these very people to stop overstating the effect.

.   .   .   .

If "curbing the Court" is not a constructive way of dealing with the nation's crime problem, what can be done? I would suggest three possible promising lines for change in dealing with the problems of crime.

First, we need to recognize that most defendants plead guilty, and thus, in the great majority of criminal cases, the crucial question is not whether the defendant committed a crime, but what should happen to him as a result of his conviction. . . .

. . . .

We are thus losing our best opportunity to use the criminal system to reduce crime. We have identified somebody who is a potential future criminal (most crimes are committed by persons who have committed prior crimes), and in many cases we have identified him early in what may turn out to be a long and destructive criminal career. We have an opportunity to try to deal with him intelligently at that point, to devote some major resources to deciding what he needs.

. . . .

The second major change we might consider is the way we deal with those who are convicted. . . .

On the hard-nosed view: We know very little about the deterrent effect of the possibility of a serious penalty. And since we are not really prepared to take every defendant out of circulation for the rest of his life, they are going to be released at some point. If we release them more dangerous than when they went into prison, we have not done much with the problem of public safety.

The therapist's view has not turned out to be much more promising. A recent California experiment took four groups of prisoners, 600 each. It offered three of these groups different kinds of intensive group counseling; the fourth group got the same prison treatment as the other three, except no group counseling. When they were all through, and had been followed up for five years, it turned out that there were no significant differences in the recidivism rates of the four groups.

Perhaps this suggests that maybe we should experiment with doing as little as posssible in as many cases as possible. . . .

. . . .

More important than trying to take out of the system those cases that should not be there is to recognize how little the system itself can do in dealing with the problem of crime and to focus more on what broadly has been called prevention.

. . . .

Simply put, this means that until we are willing to give poor people a stake in law and in order and in justice, we can expect crime to increase. The best hope of crime control lies not in better police, more convictions, longer sentences, better prisons. It lies in job training, jobs and the assurance of adequate income; schools that respond to the needs of their students; the resources and help to plan a family and hold it together; a decent place to live, and an opportunity to guide one's own life and to participate in guiding the life of the community.

.   .   .   .

Wilson

The role of court restrictions on the use of the police as a device for deterring, though surely not eliminating, street crime has to do with the point at which the police officer ceases to deter crime simply by his presence or discourage criminals by his questioning, but instead begins to set in motion the train of events that will lead to a person's being arrested and charged.

The *Miranda* decision holds that once a person is in custody, he must be warned of his rights, and I believe, for one, that it is entirely proper that he be warned of his rights. But at what point does custody begin? At what point does a casual questioning on the street of a suspicious person, asking him to identify himself and to give an account of his intentions and his activities—when does that end and when does an arrest begin?

I think it is extremely important for the police to have, under a carefully drawn statute, the right to stop and question citizens about their activities and their place of residence. I believe this is one way the police, without seriously infringing on our right of free movement, can help make the streets safer for all of us.

.   .   .   .

Let me turn now to the problem of the detection and apprehension of persons alleged already to have committed a crime. There have been a number of studies to see if the police were being inhibited by the rules of evidence that were being laid down by the Supreme Court. These studies are not clear-cut in their findings, but I think it is fair to say that on the whole they do not show any substantial loss in convictions as the result of the police being instructed to warn the suspect of his rights—the right to an attorney, the right to a court-appointed attorney if he cannot afford one, the right to remain silent, and the like.

One reason for this is that in many cases the warning is made in a perfunctory way, or perhaps not made at all, and the person is not adequately apprised of his rights. But there is also a large number of cases in which the warning is made in a serious way and the suspect chooses knowingly to waive his rights.

A study published in the *Yale Law Journal* suggests that in the case of the New Haven Police Department neither the investigating detectives nor the law-school observers were of the opinion, after examining a large number of cases, that the warnings had inhibited the giving of confessions, or that the confessions had been necessary for conviction.

It is important when talking about the role of confessions in convictions to distinguish among kinds of crimes. I think that the role of confession may be extremely important in solving burglaries and other crimes of stealth where there is no witness to the crime. Confessions may be especially important in implicating accomplices. Confessions may be important in crimes of a consensual nature, where, of course, there is no complaining witness. But in street crimes there usually is a witness, a victim who was confronted face-to-face—or sometimes back-to-front.

Here the problem is usually first getting the witness or victim to report the crime to the police. Even with robberies, half are not reported to the police at all. The second problem, after the person reports the crime, is getting his cooperation in making an identification of such suspects as the police may turn up. This again is not an easy task.

I think the chief difficulty in making good cases against persons committing street crimes lies with us, the citizens, in not reporting crimes, or, when the crime is reported and a suspect is identified, in telling the police that we don't want to get involved and that we hope they'll understand if we don't come down there. That kind of citizen noncooperation with the police seems to me a far more serious impediment to law enforcement than most appellate court decisions in this area.

.   .   .   .

I know that a lot of crime will occur no matter what we do. But I also know we cannot hold the police—or the courts—responsible for the fact that the crime that does occur is committed by people who have committed similar crimes in the past. I hold us responsible for that. I hold us responsible for not asking our state legislators to take their correctional programs more seriously. I hold us responsible for backing law and order with bumper stickers but not money. I hold us responsible for insisting that the only way to deal with offenders is to lock them up in some bucolic retreat behind high walls in the countryside, not recognizing that if we isolate them from the community their attitude toward the community will wreak a terrible price on us when, as they will be eventually, they are released.

.   .   .   .

Chapter Three

Church and State:
The Role of Religion in the
American Constitutional System

The First Amendment of the U.S. Constitution contains two clauses often referred to as the "Freedom of Religion" aspect of the Bill of Rights.

Congress shall make no law respecting the establishment of religion
or prohibiting the free exercise thereof. . . .

As with other parts of the Bill of Rights, this restriction of governmental action has been made applicable to the states through the Fourteenth Amendment. This, in itself, is a source of conflict. The history of America is a history closely linked with religion; repeatedly the Supreme Court, Congress, the President and the public have emphasized this connection. Conversely, pluralistic America takes pride in its diversity—social, political and religious. This diversity implies acceptance of all religious beliefs—or of no beliefs at all. The question then becomes: how can government be kept out of religious activities, thereby allowing diversity to develop, without, at the same time, denying the role of religious belief in our heritage?

Three approaches are possible. The first is that as long as no one religion is given a *preferred position* relative to other religions, the state should be free to give aid and encouragement. Alternatively, it is argued that there must be a *wall of separation*, a strong and high wall, between government and the church. A third approach is that governments should not act either to benefit or to burden any religion; *neutrality* is the key. Generally, in recent times, the Supreme Court has accepted the latter two alternatives in its decisions.

The issue of the role of religion in the state is one of the most sensitive areas with which the Court must deal. For one thing, it is an area in which emotions play an important part. Moreover, the Court is caught in a paradox, for by supervising state action under the establishment clause, the Court frequently appears to interfere with the free exercise of religion, at least the free exercise of the majority. The Justices have attempted repeatedly to distinguish the two clauses in order to avoid this conflict. If governmental compulsion is involved, the free exercise clause has been violated; however, any direct or indirect governmental aid to particular religions is sufficient to constitute a violation of the establishment clause.

Another problem that the Court could face (and which many critics fear) involves those religious elements which appear in virtually all of the ceremonial aspects of American political life. The President-elect traditionally uses a Bible to take the oath of office. The Congress opens its meetings with a prayer. The coins of the United States have inscribed on them "In God We Trust." The Court itself opens its sessions with "God save the United States and this Honorable Court." Mr. Justice Douglas, concurring in the *Engel* case, acknowledged the problem:

> What New York does on the opening of its public schools is what we do when we open court. Our marshal has from the beginning announced the convening of the court and then added "God save the United States and this honorable court.". . .
> What New York does on the opening of its public schools is what each House of Congress does at the opening of each day's business. . . .
> . . . Yet for me the principle is the same, no matter how briefly the prayer is said, for in each of the instances given the person praying is a public official on the public payroll, performing a religious exercise in a governmental institution.

The critics of the Court fear Mr. Justice Douglas' approach might become the view of the majority on the Supreme Court.

Shortly after World War II, the Court permitted state governments to use public funds for the busing of children to parochial schools (*Everson* v. *Board of Education*, 1947). To justify such state action, the Court argued that the state law "does no more than provide a general program to help parents get their children, regardless of the religion, safely and expeditiously to and from accredited schools." The state was aiding the child, not the church. In 1952 the Justices ruled that public schools could release children early for religious training, but the training could not utilize public facilities (*Zorach v. Clausen,* 1952). With these beginnings, it appeared that the majority on the Court was giving significant weight to America's religious heritage and in practice following a "no preferred" position approach.

However, in 1962, in the landmark case of *Engel* v. *Vitale,* the high court struck down as a form of establishment a nondenominational prayer written by the New York State Regents. Religion was "too personal, too sacred, too holy, to permit its 'unhallowed perversion' by a civil magistrate." The state and church must remain separate. With the *Engel* decision the Court created the intense political debate with which this issue has been marked ever since. The Justices appeared to be threatening America's religious heritage.

The fears of the anti-Court groups were not dispelled when, in *Abington School District* v. *Schempp* (1963), the Court majority declared unconstitutional as a form of state establishment the practice of Bible reading in public schools. The Court moved from a "wall of separation" doctrine in *Engel* to "neutrality" in religious matters. The problem of a possible conflict between the establishment and free exercise clauses prompted the new approach. The establishment clause aspect of neutrality means that there can be no fusion of governmental and religious functions. In addition, for the Justices,

> . . . a further reason for neutrality is found in the Free Exercise Clause, which recognizes the value of religious training, teaching and observance and, more particularly, the right of every person to freely choose his own course with reference thereto, free of any compulsion from the state. This the Free Exercise Clause guarantees. Thus, as we have seen, the two clauses may overlap.

The concept of neutrality, according to Justice Tom Clark, who wrote the Court's opinion, prevents a conflict "with the majority's right to free exercise of religion." The state cannot deny to anyone the right to practice his religion.* Conversely, the state cannot, through majority rule, impose any set of beliefs—however broad—on all of its citizens. Thus, this approach neither grants any benefits nor imposes any burdens. Few of the Court's critics were convinced that neutrality solved the problem of free exercise vs. establishment. The following readings illustrate the dissatisfaction.

---

*See Philip B. Kurland, *Religion and the Law* (Chicago: Aldine Publishing Co., 1962) and H. J. Abraham, *Freedom and the Court* (New York: Oxford University Press, 1967).

The Court may yet adopt alternatives in future cases or it may choose to expand the concept of neutrality. However it chooses to handle conflicts in the future, the fact still remains that its recent decisions have satisfied few. Congress has taken the lead in attempting to undo the decision in *Engel* and *Schempp*. Most of these attempts have been through resolutions to amend the constitution and to influence public opinion. Although amendments have yet to be proposed, the latter course has borne fruit. Compliance in this area of constitutional standards has been poor. Public schools in many areas have chosen to defy the Court, knowing that the Court is virtually helpless to enforce its decisions. Unless such defiance is itself challenged by citizens, it may continue. In the long run, the decisions of the Court are effective only if the people observe them. The Justices have no troops to enforce their decisions. Should the President ignore decisions, should Congress fail to implement them through legislation, should the states wish to defy rulings and should the people continue outlawed practices, the Court is helpless. This has been the case with the prayers and Bible reading issue in many regions of the United States.

"Too Personal, Too Sacred, Too Holy. . . ." (1962)*

Engel v. *Vitale*

The following case begins the contemporary furor over the meaning of the religion clauses of the First Amendment. Reactions to the *Engel* case varied from Alabama Congressman George W. Andrews' comment that the Court had "put the Negroes in the schools and now they've driven God out" to Evangelist Billy Graham's statement that the Constitution meant "that we were to have freedom *of* religion, not freedom *from* religion." Justice Hugo Black delivered the opinion of the Court.

The respondent Board of Education of Union Free School District No. 9, New Hyde Park, New York, acting in its official capacity under state law, directed the School District's principal to cause the following prayer to be said aloud by each class in the presence of a teacher at the beginning of each school day:

---

*370 U.S. 421.

Almighty God, we acknowledge our dependence upon Thee, and we beg Thy blessings upon us, our parents, our teachers and our country.

This daily procedure was adopted on the recommendation of the State Board of Regents, a governmental agency created by the State Constitution to which the New York Legislature has granted broad supervisory, executive, and legislative powers over the State's public school system. These state officials composed the prayer which they recommended and published as a part of their "Statement on Moral and Spiritual Training in the Schools," saying: "We believe that this Statement will be subscribed to by all men and women of good will, and we call upon all of them to aid in giving life to our program."

... [T]he parents of ten pupils brought this action in a New York State Court insisting that use of this official prayer in the public schools was contrary to the beliefs, religions, or religious practices of both themselves and their children. Among other things, these parents challenged the constitutionality of both the state law authorizing the School District to direct the use of prayer in public schools and the School District's regulation ordering the recitation of this particular prayer on the ground that these actions of official governmental agencies violate that part of the First Amendment of the Federal Constitution which commands that "Congress shall make no law respecting an establishment of religion"—a command which was "made applicable to the State of New York by the Fourteenth Amendment of the said Constitution."

We think that by using its public school system to encourage recitation of the Regents' prayer, the State of New York has adopted a practice wholly inconsistent with the Establishment Clause. There can, of course, be no doubt that New York's program of daily classroom invocation of God's blessings as prescribed in the Regents' prayer is a religious activity. It is a solemn avowal of divine faith and supplication for the blessings of the Almighty.

The petitioners contend among other things that the state laws requiring or permitting use of the Regents' prayer must be struck down as a violation of the Establishment Clause because that prayer was composed by governmental officials as a part of a governmental program to further religious beliefs. ... We agree with that contention since we think that the constitutional prohibition against laws respecting an establishment of religion must at least mean that in this country it is no part of the business of government to compose official prayers for any group of the American people to recite as a part of a religious program carried on by government.

It is a matter of history that this very practice of establishing governmentally composed prayers for religious services was one of the reasons which caused many of our early colonists to leave England and seek religious freedom in America.

. . . .

By the time of the adoption of the Constitution, our history shows that there was a widespread awareness among many Americans of the dangers of a union of Church and State. The First Amendment was added to the Constitution to stand as a guarantee that neither the power nor the prestige of the Federal Government would be used to control, support or influence the kinds of prayer the American people can say—that the people's religions must not be subjected to the pressures of government for change each time a new political administration is elected to office. Under that Amendment's prohibition against governmental establishment of religion, as reinforced by the provisions of the Fourteenth Amendment, government in this country, be it state or federal, is without power to prescribe by law any particular form of prayer which is to be used as an official prayer in carrying on any program of governmentally sponsored religious activity.

There can be no doubt that New York's state prayer program officially establishes the religious beliefs embodied in the Regents' prayer. Neither the fact that the prayer may be denominationally neutral, nor the fact that its observance on the part of the students is voluntary can serve to free it from the limitations of the Establishment Clause, as it might from the Free Exercise Clause, of the First Amendment, both of which are operative against the States by virtue of the Fourteenth Amendment. Although these two clauses may in certain instances overlap, they forbid two quite different kinds of governmental encroachment upon religious freedom. The Establishment Clause, unlike the Free Exercise Clause, does not depend upon any showing of direct governmental compulsion and is violated by the enactment of laws which establish an official religion whether those laws operate directly to coerce nonobserving individuals or not. When the power, prestige and financial support of government is placed behind a particular religious belief, the indirect coercive pressure upon religious minorities to conform to the prevailing officially approved religion is plain. But the purposes underlying the Establishment Clause go much further than that. Its first and most immediate purpose rested on the belief that a union of government and religion tends to destroy government and to degrade religion. The Establishment Clause thus stands as an expression of principle on the part of the Founders of our Constitution that religion is too personal, too sacred, too holy, to permit its "unhallowed perversion" by a civil magistrate. Another purpose of the Establishment Clause rested upon an awareness of the historical fact that governmentally established religions and religious persecutions go hand in hand.... The New York laws officially prescribing the Regents' prayer are inconsistent with both the purposes of the Establishment Clause and with the Establishment Clause itself.

It has been argued that to apply the Constitution in such a way as to prohibit state laws respecting an establishment of religious services in public schools is to indicate a hostility toward religion or toward prayer. Nothing, of course, could be more wrong. The history of man is inseparable from the history of religion. And perhaps it is not too much to say that since the beginning of that history many people have devoutly believed that "More things are wrought by prayer than this world dreams of." It was doubtless largely due to men who believed this that there grew up a sentiment that caused men to leave the cross-currents of officially established state religions and religious persecution in Europe and come to this country filled with the hope that they could find a place in which they could pray when they pleased to the God of their faith in the language they chose. And there were men of this same faith in the power of prayer who led the fight for adoption of our Constitution and also for our Bill of Rights with the very guarantees of religious freedom that forbid the sort of governmental activity which New York has attempted here. It is neither sacrilegious nor antireligious to say that each separate government in this country should stay out of the business of writing or sanctioning official prayers and leave that purely religious function to the people themselves and to those the people choose to look to for religious guidance. To those who may subscribe to the view that because the Regents' official prayer is so brief and general there can be no danger to religious freedom in its governmental establishment, however, it may be appropriate to say in the words of James Madison, the author of the First Amendment:

[I]t is proper to take alarm at the first experiment on our liberties. . . . Who does not see that the same authority which can establish Christianity, in exclusion of all other Religions, may establish with the same ease any particular sect of Christians, in exclusion of all other Sects? That the same authority which can force a citizen to contribute three pence only of his property for the support of any one establishment, may force him to conform to any other establishment in all cases whatsoever?

The judgment of the Court of Appeals of New York is reversed and the cause remanded for further proceedings not inconsistent with this opinion.

.   .   .   .

Justice Potter Stewart dissented in the following opinion.

... The Court today decides that in permitting this brief nondenominational prayer the school board has violated the Constitution of the United States. I think this decision is wrong.

.   .   .   .

With all respect, I think the Court has misapplied a great constitutional principle. I cannot see how an "official religion" is established by letting those who want to say a prayer say it. On the contrary, I think that to deny the wish of these school children to join in reciting this prayer is to deny them the opportunity of sharing in the spiritual heritage of our Nation. . . .

.   .   .   .

I do not believe that this Court, or the Congress, or the President has by the actions and practices I have mentioned established an "official religion" in violation of the Constitution. And I do not believe the State of New York has done so in this case. What each has done has been to recognize and to follow the deeply entrenched and highly cherished spiritual traditions of our Nation—traditions which come down to us from those who almost two hundred years ago avowed their "firm reliance on the Protection of Divine Providence" when they proclaimed the freedom and independence of this brave new world.

Opinion Leaders and Prayers in Public Schools (1962)*

The following collection is illustrative of the initial reactions to the *Engel* case.

The Congress should at once submit an amendment to the Constitution which establishes the right to religious devotion in all governmental agencies—national, state or local.

Former President Herbert Hoover

. . . .

I realize, of course, that the Declaration of Independence ante-dates the Constitution, but the fact remains that the Declaration was our certificate of national birth. It specifically asserts that we as in-dividuals possess certain rights as an endowment from our common creator—a religious concept.

Former President Dwight D. Eisenhower

. . . .

I am shocked and frightened that the Supreme Court has declared unconstitutional a simple and voluntary declaration of belief in God by public school children. The decision strikes at the very heart of the Godly tradition in which America's children have for so long been raised.

Cardinal Spellman of New York

. . . .

The recitation of prayers in the public schools, which is tantamount to the teaching of prayer, is not in conformity with the spirit of the American concept of the separation of church and state. All the re-ligious groups in this country will best advance their respective faiths by adherence to this principle.

New York Board of Rabbis

. . . .

This is another step toward the secularization of the United States. Followed to its logical conclusion, we will have to take the chaplains out of the armed forces, prayers cannot be said in Congress, and the President cannot put his hand on the Bible when he takes the oath of office. The framers of our Constitution meant we were to have freedom of religion, not freedom from religion.

Evangelist Billy Graham

. . . .

I am surprised that the Court has extended to an obviously non-sectarian prayer the prohibition against "the establishment of religion" which was clearly intended by our forefathers to bar official status to any particular denomination or sect.

Episcopal Bishop James A. Pike

. . . .

All parties agreed that the prayer was religious in nature. This being so, it ran contrary to the First Amendment—which is well grounded in history and has served to save the United States from religious strife.

Representative Emanuel Celler (D., New York)

.   .   .   .

It is important that people not be misled by distorted statements about the decision. The Supreme Court has nowhere in its decision denied belief in God, prayer, religious songs, Bible reading, or any other religious belief or practice.

Rabbi Albert M. Lewis, Los Angeles

.   .   .   .

Can it be that we, too, are ready to embrace the foul concept of atheism. . . . Is this not in fact the first step on the road to prompting atheistic and agnostic beliefs? . . . Somebody is tampering with America's soul. I leave to you who that somebody is.

Senator Robert C. Byrd (D., W. Va.)

.   .   .   .

For some years now the members of the Supreme Court have persisted in reading alien meanings into the Constitution of the United States. . . . they have sought, in effect, to change our form of government. But never in the wildest of their excesses . . . have they gone as far as they did on yesterday.

Senator Herman Talmadge (D., Ga.)

.   .   .   .

Be it resolved that the conference urge the Congress of the United States to propose an amendment to the constitution of the United States that will make clear and beyond challenge the acknowledgment of our nation and people of their faith in God and permit the free and voluntary participation in prayer in our public schools.

Resolution of the Annual Governors' Conference, July 3, 1962.[1]

President Kennedy and Prayers in School (1962)*

President Kennedy's position concerning religion and the state was especially sensitive considering the fact that he was the first Catholic President in America's history. His religion had been an issue with some

---

[1] The resolution was approved by the Governors' Conference with only Governor Rockefeller, abstaining. The New York Governor commented: "I shall abstain from the endorsement of any hasty action by the Governors relating to amendment of the U.S. Constitution." *New York Times*, July 4, 1962, p. 8.

*Excerpts from President Kennedy's news conference. John F. Kennedy, *Public Papers of the President of the U.S.: 1962* (U.S.: Government Printing Office, 1963), pp. 510–511.

people in the Presidential campaign of 1960. However, as the following reading indicates, he remained consistent with his initial response to the Church issue—one's religious beliefs were a personal and private matter.

Q. Mr. President, in the furor over the Supreme Court's decision on prayer in the schools, some members of Congress have been introducing legislation for constitutional amendments specifically to sanction prayer or religious exercise in the schools. Can you give us your opinion of the decision itself and of these moves of the Congress to circumvent it?

THE PRESIDENT: I haven't seen the measures in the Congress and you would have to make a determination of what the language was and what effect it would have on the first amendment. The Supreme Court has made its judgment, and a good many people obviously will disagree with it. Others will agree with it. But I think that it is important for us if we are going to maintain our constitutional principle that we support the Supreme Court decisions even when we may not agree with them.

In addition, we have in this case a very easy remedy and that is to pray ourselves. And I would think that it would be a welcome reminder to every American family that we can pray a good deal more at home, we can attend our churches with a good deal more fidelity, and we can make the true meaning of prayer much more important in the lives of all of our children. That power is very much open to us. And I would hope that as a result of this decision that all American parents will intensify their efforts at home, and the rest of us will support the Constitution and the responsibility of the Supreme Court in interpreting it, which is theirs, and given to them by the Constitution.

A "Religion of Secularism"? (1963)*

School District of Abington Township v. *Schempp*

In the *Schempp* case the Court attempted to deal directly with the growing conflict between the two religion clauses of the First Amendment. By preventing public schools from being involved in a voluntary program of Bible reading, because this activity is in violation of the

---

*374 U.S. 203.

establishment clause, the Justices may be preventing the majority of the people from freely exercising their religion. Religious training, teaching and observance are certainly part of America's religious heritage. Why should not the schools be involved in this tradition? The concept of "neutrality" provides one answer to the problem of maintaining a balance between the establishment and free exercise clauses. Justice Tom Clark delivered the opinion of the Court.

"The government is neutral, [in religious matters] and, while protecting all, it prefers none, and it disparages none."

. . . .

The wholesome "neutrality" of which this Court's cases speak stems from a recognition of the teachings of history that powerful sects or groups might bring about a fusion of governmental and religious functions or a concert or dependency about a fusion of governmental and religious functions or a concert or dependency of one upon the other to the end that official support of the state or federal government would be placed behind the tenets of one or all orthodoxies. This the establishment clause prohibits. And a further reason for neutrality is found in the free exercise clause, which recognizes the value of religious training, teaching and observance and, more particularly, the right of every person to freely choose his own course with reference thereto, free of any compulsion from the state. This the free exercise clause guarantees. Thus, as we have seen, the two clauses may overlap.

. . . The establishment clause has been directly considered by this Court eight times in the past score of years and, with only one Justice dissenting on the point, it has consistently held that the clause withdrew all legislative power respecting religious belief of the expression thereof. The test may be stated as follows: what are the purpose and the primary effect of the enactment? If either is the advancement or inhibition of religion then the enactment exceeds the scope of legislative power as circumscribed by the Constitution. That is to say that to withstand the strictures of the establishment clause there must be a secular legislative purpose and a primary effect that neither advances nor inhibits religion. . . .

. . . the State contends . . . that the [Bible reading] program is an effort to extend its benefits to all public school children without regard to their religious belief. Included within its secular purposes, it says, are the promotion of moral values, the contradiction to the materialistic trends of our times, the perpetuation of our institutions and the

teaching of literature. . . . But even if its purpose is not strictly religious, it is sought to be accomplished through readings, without comment, from the Bible. Surely the place of the Bible as an instrument
of religion cannot be gainsaid, and the State's recognition of the
pervading religious character of the ceremony is evident from the
rule's specific permission of the alternative use of the Catholic Douay
version as well as the recent amendment permitting nonattendance at
the exercises. None of these factors is consistent with the contention
that the Bible is here used either as an instrument for nonreligious
moral inspiration or as a reference for the teaching of secular subjects.

. . . .

It is insisted that unless these religious exercises are permitted a
"religion of secularism" is established in the schools. We agree of course
that the State may not establish a "religion of secularism" in the sense
of affirmatively opposing or showing hostility to religion, thus "pre-
ferring those who believe in no religion over those who do believe." . . .
We do not agree, however, that this decision in any sense has that
effect. . . . Nothing we have said here indicates that such study of the
Bible or of religion, when presented objectively as part of a secular
program of education, may not be effected consistent with the First
Amendment. But the exercises here do not fall into those categories.
They are religious exercises, required by the States in violation of the
command of the First Amendment that the Government maintain
strict neutrality, neither aiding nor opposing religion.

Finally, we cannot accept that the concept of neutrality, which
does not permit a State to require a religious exercise even with the
consent of the majority of those affected, collides with the majority's
right to free exercise of religion. While the free exercise clause clearly
prohibits the use of state action to deny the rights of free exercise to
anyone, it has never meant that a majority could use the machinery
of the State to practice its beliefs. . . .

The place of religion in our society is an exalted one, achieved
through a long tradition of reliance on the home, the church and the
inviolable citadel of the individual heart and mind. We have come to
recognize through bitter experience that it is not within the power of
government to invade that citadel, whether its purpose or effect be
to aid or oppose, to advance or retard. In the relationship between
man and religion, the state is firmly committed to a position of neutrality. Though the application of that rule requires interpretation of
a delicate sort, the rule itself is clearly and concisely stated in the
words of the First Amendment. . . .

Justice William O. Douglas concurred as follows.

Establishment of a religion can be achieved in several ways. The church and state can be one; the church may control the state or the state may control the church; or the relationship may take one of several possible forms of a working arrangement between the two bodies. Under all of these arrangements the church typically has a place in the state's budget, and church law usually governs such matters as baptism, marriage, divorce and separation, at least for its members and sometimes for the entire body politic. Education, too, is usually high on the priority list of church interests. In the past schools were often made the exclusive responsibility of the church. . . .

The vice of all such arrangements under the Establishment Clause is that the state is lending its assistance to a church's efforts to gain and keep adherents. Under the First Amendment it is strictly a matter for the individual and his church as to what church he will belong to and how much support, in the way of belief, time, activity or money, he will give to it. . . .

In these cases we have no coercive religious exercise aimed at making the students conform. The prayers announced are not compulsory, . . . so the vices of the present regimes are different.

These regimes violate the Establishment Clause in two different ways. In each case the State is conducting a religious exercise; and, as the Court holds, that cannot be done without violating the "neutrality" required of the State by the balance of power between individual, church and state that has been struck by the First Amendment. But the Establishment Clause is not limited to precluding the State itself from conducting religious exercises. It also forbids the State to employ its facilities or funds in a way that gives any church, or all churches, greater strength in our society than it would have by relying on its members alone. Thus, the present regimes must fall under that clause for the additional reason that public funds, though small in amount, are being used to promote a religious exercise. Through the mechanism of the State, all of the people are being required to finance a religious exercise that only some of the people want and that violates the sensibilities of others.

.   .   .   .

Justice William Brennan concurred as follows.

While it is not, of course, appropriate for this Court to decide questions not presently before it, I venture to suggest that religious exercises in the public schools present a unique problem. For not every envolvement of religion in public life violates the Establishment Clause. Our decision in these cases does not clearly forecast anything about the constitutionality of other types of interdependence between religious and other public institutions.

. . . What the Framers meant to foreclose, and what our decisions under the Establishment Clause have forbidden, are those involvements of religious with secular institutions which (a) serve the essentially religious activities of religious institutions; (b) employ the organs of government for essentially religious purposes; or (c) use essentially religious means to serve governmental ends, where secular means would suffice. . . .

.   .   .   .

Justice Potter Stewart dissented in the following opinion.

.   .   .   .

. . . there is involved in these cases a substantial free exercise claim on the part of those who affirmatively desire to have their children's school day open with the reading of passages from the Bible.

.   .   .   .

. . . For a compulsory state educational system so structures a child's life that if religious exercises are held to be an impermissible activity in schools, religion is placed at an artificial and state-created disadvantage. Viewed in this light, permission of such exercises for those who want them is necessary if the schools are truly to be neutral in the matter of religion. And a refusal to permit religious exercises thus is seen, not as the realization of state neutrality, but rather as the establishment of a religion of secularism, or at the least, as government support of the beliefs of those who think that religious exercises should be conducted only in private.

Billy Graham Voices Shock Over *Schempp* Decision (1963)*

The popular reaction to the *Schempp* decision was generally quiet with the exception of Reverend Billy Graham. Only one year had passed between the *Engel* and *Schempp* decisions but the furor over the Court's intervention into this area was dying down. This was due in part to

---

*New York Times, June 18, 1963, p. 27.

churchmen persuading their congregations of the wisdom of the Court's decision. Also the Court's decision in *Schempp* was a carefully written opinion by Justice Clark, a Presbyterian, who had support from Justice Brennan, a Catholic and Justice Goldberg, a Jew.

I am shocked at the Supreme Court's decision. Prayers and Bible reading have been a part of American public school life since the Pilgrims landed at Plymouth Rock.

Now a Supreme Court in 1963 says our fathers were wrong all these years. In my opinion, it is the Supreme Court that is wrong.

At a time when moral decadence is evident on every hand, when race tension is mounting, when the threat of Communism is growing, when terrifying new weapons of destruction are being created, we need more religion, not less.

Eighty per cent of the American people want Bible reading and prayer in the schools. Why should the majority be so severely penalized by the protests of a handful?

Congress and Prayers in School (1963)*
The Becker Amendment

Congress reacted to the *Engel* and *Schempp* cases with the introduction of over a hundred resolutions to amend the Constitution. Congressman Becker's proposal is representative of these resolutions.

Nothing in this Constitution shall be deemed to prohibit the offering, reading from, or listening to prayers or Biblical Scriptures, if participation therein is on a voluntary basis, in any governmental or public school, institution or place.

Nothing in this Constitution shall be deemed to prohibit making reference to belief in, reliance upon, or invoking the aid of God or a

---

*Proposed by Representative Frank J. Becker (R.-N.Y.).

Although there seemed to be wide public support for the Becker Amendment Congress delayed action and the Amendment remained in committee. House Joint Resolution 9. Introduced January 9, 1963.

Supreme Being in any governmental or public document, proceeding, activity, ceremony, school, institution, or place, or upon any coinage, currency, or obligation of the United States.

Nothing in this Article shall constitute an establishment of religion.

Congressman Becker Answers the American Jewish Congress (1964)*

Addressing the House Judiciary Committee, the New York Congressman made the following points:

1. On the statement that the amendment "threatens the integrity of the Bill of Rights," Becker asked:

"Are the people of the United States to be compelled to submit to a nine-man oligarchy and deprived of their right to dissent or disagree with Supreme Court decisions? . . . How can . . . the Bill of Rights be imperiled by the exercise of those rights?"

2. On the statement that the amendment "threatens the principle of church-state separation," Becker said:

"Down through the years, devotional exercises in schools, graduation ceremonies, inaugurations, Fourth of July celebrations, etc., have been a fundamental part of what we might refer to as 'Americana.' The Pledge of Allegiance, the Star-Spangled Banner, Washington's Farewell Address, the Declaration of Independence, public documents . . . all fitted into this pattern of America's tradition of faith.

"Why now at this late date, knowing these exercises have only brought strength and goodness to our people, are we to be challenged and denied this humble right . . .?

. . . .

"I know of no man advocating this formula for the protection of devotional exercises who has even the faintest desire to weaken the

---

*The following excerpts were taken from Congressman Frank J. Becker's testimony before the House Judiciary Committee. The American Jewish Congress opposed the Becker Amendment for the reasons outlined in the Congressman's remarks. Hearings on School Prayers, House Committee on the Judiciary, 88th Congress, 2d. Sess. (1964).

traditional opposition which our people have to the combining of church and state."

3. On the statement that this proposal "threatens the principle of religious freedom," Becker maintained:

"I yield to no one in my support of religious freedom, and I can remember no dilemma faced by any student during my years in school when the Lord's Prayer was said every day I attended school. No one suffered a dilemma when passages were read from the King James' Version of the Bible, although I am a Roman Catholic. There were Catholics, Protestants, and Jews in my school, but we never thought of one another as such.

. . . .

4. On the statement that the amendment "threatens the integrity of the public school system," Becker disagreed:

"I think it would be extremely difficult to find a situation where sectarian strife was introduced into a public school because of a prayer issue." Becker reported that "a handful of people" had raised the prayer issue, and said that "the two Supreme Court decisions [on school prayer] have created more disunity among our people—in fact, almost the first disunity among our people—concerning such matters." The Congressman raised this question: "Are we to become so illogical as to believe that the way to promote unity among our people is to outlaw God, step on God, ridicule God, and deny God in our public institutions in a land where we owe this same God a debt of gratitude for the abundance which has been bestowed among us?"

5. On the final statement that the proposed amendment "is not helpful, but rather hurtful to religion," Congressman Becker said this:

"The school is an educational organization, and no book has been more a part of our civilization than the Holy Bible. . . . Are we to permit a little handful of oversensitive atheists to carve out of our educational system an understanding of the book and the document which has meant more to our way of life than all the other volumes combined—The Holy Bible."

Becker said that in a sense he was "indebted to the American Jewish Congress . . . because I believe that they have summarized the logic of the opposition as completely as any group or any organization whose comment on the subject has been brought to my attention. We should all be thankful that we live in a land where each of us can disagree on subjects such as this without in any way imperiling or sacrificing our personal liberty."

The Prayer Amendment Issue Continues (1967)*

Following the Court decisions in *Engel* and *Schempp* Congress proposed a number of Amendments to allow prayers and Bible reading in public schools. Although the decisions were handed down in 1962 and 1963, the efforts for Congressional action continue. Congresswoman Charlotte Reid, (D., Ill.) added her voice to those who wish to "correct" the Court's rulings.

Mr. Speaker, during these past few days I have presented several statements here in the House of Representatives, expressing my deep concern over the crime, rioting, burning, and looting which are raging throughout our land. . . .

Everyone is asking "Why is this happening here? Where have we failed? What are the causes of this decline in morality and respect for law and order?". . . .

Today I want to remind you also that many of those involved in criminal activities and rioting, looting, and destruction of other people's property are the very young and ask you to ponder whether it is mere coincidence that the criminal activities of these young people— even though admittedly a minority—have risen so greatly since the Supreme Court decisions which to all effects and purposes have banned prayer and Bible reading or any reference to a deity in our schools. I just wonder how many of these young people who have resorted to criminal activities have even read these words from the Ten Commandments contained in the Holy Bible:

Thou shalt not kill; Thou shalt not steal; Thou shalt not covet thy neighbor's house . . . nor anything that is thy neighbor's.

Ours is a nation founded under God—and has grown to greatness under God—and our history shows that prayers are an integral part of our heritage.

. . . .

On July 27, President Johnson spoke to the Nation over television and radio on "Law and Order in America"—ending such statement with these words:

Let us pray for the day when "mercy and truth are met together; righteousness and peace have kissed each other." Let us pray . . . Let us then act in the Congress, in the city halls, and in every community, so that this great land of ours, may truly be "one Nation under God . . . with liberty and justice for all."

Congressional Record, August 9, 1967, pp. H10228-9.

On that same day, July 27, our President issued a proclamation calling for a National Day of Prayer for Reconciliation—including these words:

We pray to Almighty God, the Author of our liberty, for hearts free from hate, so that our Nation can be free from bitterness. We pray for strength to build together so that disorder may cease, progress steadily continue, and justice prosper.

It is incongruous to me that on that very same day—July 27—when our President was calling upon the help of God and urging our citizens to pray for guidance, that a U.S. court of appeals tribunal—by a 2-to-1 decision—should overrule a previous court decision and decide that kindergarten students in De Kalb Community Unit School District 428, which is in my congressional district, would no longer be allowed to recite the following verse:

We thank you for the flowers so sweet.
We thank you for the food we eat.
We thank you for the birds that sing.
We thank you, God, for everything.[1]

The kindergarten teacher told the court that she used the verse to teach good citizenship and thankfulness. The two justices who ruled against recitation of this verse held, however, that:

"The secular purposes of the verse were merely adjunctive and supplemental to its basic and primary purpose, which was a religious act of praising and thanking the deity."

Obviously they felt they had to make this decision because of the Supreme Court rulings which overturned the historical practices of permitting voluntary prayer and reference to God in our public schools since the founding of our Nation, even though they apparently recognized the purpose of the verse was to make children become more grateful for the things they receive and to help them in becoming better citizens. I would also like to point out that this court battle involving this verse has been going on since 1965 upon the complaint of the parents of one child who has long since left kindergarten.

.   .   .   .

I remain convinced that the Supreme Court prayer and Bible reading decisions of 1962 and 1963 represent serious misinterpretations of that first amendment. I agree wholeheartedly with Senator Strom Thurmond's statement that:

---

[1] The Supreme Court upheld the lower court decision to which Congresswoman Reid refers. See *DeKalb County Community School District* v. *Despain*, 390 U.S. 906 (1968).

"Since the Supreme Court has ruled . . . freedom is a one-way street. The children in the public schools are free *not* to pray, but they are not free to pray even if they want to. This is freedom *from* religion, and not freedom *of* religion. . . ."

I have introduced resolutions calling for a constitutional amendment which would restore the freedom of voluntary prayer to our students in our schools. To my regret, however, I—and others who have introduced identical or similar resolutions—have been unsuccessful in our efforts to secure final and favorable congressional action. . . .

My present resolution, is identical to Senate Joint Resolution 1 introduced in the Senate by Senator Dirksen, for himself and 43 other Senators from both parties, and simply states:

"Nothing contained in this Constitution shall abridge the right of persons lawfully assembled, in any public building which is supported in whole or in part through the expenditure of public funds, to participate in nondenominational prayer."

When I testified in support of such a prayer amendment in 1964, I stated my feeling that:

"To deny our youth, their teachers, and their counsellors the privilege of a communal exercise of their allegiance to God as well as to Country is a rejection of our most constant source of power and strength."

I also pointed out that we live in a season of increasing immorality and warned that:

"Any diminution of emphasis on individual, moral, and spiritual responsibilities can only further reduce our level of integrity and increase our rate of crime."

Today, I respectfully call upon the honorable chairman of the House Committee on the Judiciary to take prompt action in earnest consideration of reporting the prayer amendment. I also express my sincere hope that our President will take the lead in calling for prompt passage of the prayer amendment since he has indicated on numerous occasions that he believes in the power of prayer, faith in the Almighty God, and that ours is really "one Nation under God."

Pennsylvanians Lead School Prayer Revolt (1969)*

Another reason why some of the criticism of the high court's decisions in the area of prayers and Bible reading abated was because

---

*Ben. A. Franklin, *New York Times*, March 26, 1969, p. 1. © 1967–1969 by the New York Times Company. Reprinted with permission.

many school districts were clearly ignoring or defying the Supreme Court's rulings. Before the 1962 *Engel* case approximately 30 percent of all schools had some form of prayers or rites religious in nature. The *Schempp* decision affected 41 percent of the schools in 37 states. By 1964 it was clear that Congressman Becker's amendment would never be reported out of committee. Congress was thus prevented from acting. For those great number of schools that had given value to religious readings the only recourse was defiance. Perhaps 13 percent of the nation's public schools, including up to 50 percent in the South, were continuing devotional readings. The Supreme Court was helpless to act. It cannot enforce its decisions. Only when litigants bring cases before it can the Justices act. Compliance constitutes the cement which holds together the American constitutional system. One might ask whether the constitutional system was stronger as a result of the Bible and prayer decisions.

At 9 o'clock each morning of the school week, Miss Donna Pomella reads a passage from the Bible to her first-grade class at the Fifth Street Elementary School here.

Then after the children have bowed their heads, the pretty, dark-haired teacher leads the class in a recitation of the Lord's Prayer.

Thus is Scripture being bootlegged into the public schools of the Monongahela Valley—in direct defiance of the United States Supreme Court.

There is a special excitement to the revival of classroom devotion for the people of Clairton, for after six years of obedience they are knowingly performing an illegal if pious act. But the classroom scene here is being re-enacted inconspicuously in countless other communities where school boards have simply ignored the mandate that was handed down by the Court.

Although no precise current information is available, nearly 13 per cent of the nation's public schools—and nearly 50 per cent of the South's —were continuing devotional readings as late as 1966, according to figures compiled by Prof. Richard B. Dierenfield of Macalester College. And by all indications the practice has been spreading since then.

The Supreme Court ruled in 1963 that prescribed religious proceedings of any kind in public schools were unconstitutional . . . Like Prohibition, however, the prayer ban appears to have little popular acceptance. In Clairton, for example, many people feel that their youngsters "went to hell when God was put out of the classroom."

. . . .

In Alabama, . . . no citizen has challenged the 1927 state law requiring public school teachers to make and report daily Bible readings in class on pain of losing a day's pay for each omission.

So the law there is still on the books and is still observed as if the Supreme Court had never spoken. Similar laws prevail across the Deep South, and there are repeated signs of pressures for a Bible-reading revival elsewhere.

.   .   .   .

In 1964, the Cornwall-Lebanon joint school district in central Pennsylvania was challenged by a local citizen in the United States District Court at Lewisburg for attempting to reinstate a prescribed morning devotional period. The school board lost in a test case that seemed at the time to have settled the issue. The Supreme Court was upheld.

The state government subsequently published a seven-point guideline suggesting constitutionally appropriate alternatives to prayer that were widely accepted.

The guideline, still in effect, suggests as permissible silent meditation in the classroom and "the objective study" of the Bible "for literary and historic qualities," among other projects.

But it plainly bars prayer and Scripture reading, even where teachers have the nominal option of noncompliance, if the worship period is initiated by school authorities.

.   .   .   .

According to school officials, clergymen and lawyers familiar with the phenomenon here, much of industrial and mining western Pennsylvania is angry over the youth rebellion, over crime and permissive courts, over Negroes, taxes and welfare.

The back-to-the-Bible movement, they say, is the visible symptom of a desire to stop talking and start acting in fundamentalist terms that seem tried and true to many Americans.

It is the theory of Carmine V. Molinaro, a Connellsville lawyer and attorney for the Albert Gallatin area school district in Fayette County, that "People are mad at the Government, and since they can't get at the Federal or state government, the only government they can tackle is local government. So they are doing it."

.   .   .   .

Mr. Molinaro said he had strongly counseled his board that what they were asked to do in citizen petitions and in personal confrontations at a public meeting was unconstitutional and ill-advised.

But among the 300 angry citizens at the meeting who were press-
ing for Bible and prayer reading was William E. Duffield, an outspoken
Uniontown lawyer who was a Presidential supporter of George C.
Wallace and is president of the Fayette County Anti-Tax Protest
Committee. And the school board was apparently in no mood to invite
the wrath of that rapidly growing and militant group.

"What we have here is really a revolution in a mild sense of the
word," Mr. Molinaro said. Agreeing, Mr. Duffield commented on the
acknowledged unconstitutionality of the board's prayer decision by
declaring: "The Boston Tea Party was illegal too."

· · · · · · · · · · · · · · · · · ·

In Clairton and in Phillipsburg, on the other hand, the school
board action is being interpreted as optional for teachers but not for
the pupils. Thus, if a teacher chooses to read the Bible and have
prayers—and most reportedly do under the current emotional circumstances—objecting students would appear to have no recourse.

In any event, according to the thinking of the Supreme Court,
voluntarism adds no saving quality.

· · · · · · · · · · · · · · · · ·

At the Clairton Junior-Senior High School, a recent Student
Council survey among 201 seniors found 116 for prayer and Bible
reading, 78 for silent meditation and 7 for no classroom religious
observance at all.

The principal, Neil C. Brown, said: "Of course, I don't think there
is a Jew in this school, so there is no objection from that quarter."

· · · · · · · · · · · · · · · · ·

Two months ago, against the professional advice of its newly hired
school superintendent, Dr. Robert LaFrankie, and against the legal
advice of its attorney, the Clairton school board voted, 9 to 0, with
almost no discussion, to accede to the High School Parent-Teachers
Association's request for Bible and prayer reading.

· · · · · · · · · · · · · · · · ·

"In a time of turmoil in the country," he said in an interview,
"our parents think the loss of Bible reading in school has contributed
to the deterioration of the United States. This is not only an act of
defiance, it is an attempt to survive."

· · · · · · · · · · · · · · · · ·

The schools' act of defiance, in any case, is more a symbol of frustration than an act of constitutional nullification carrying with it a
clear-cut risk.

"What the hell," one school official said. "It's illegal, but they can't put us in jail. All they can do is get an injunction."

The Clairton school board has already decided to pay the legal costs of the court fight, if it comes.

The Pittsburgh office of the American Civil Liberties Union, which would like to locate a local plaintiff to file what it regards as "an open-and-shut lawsuit" to end Clairton's defiance, has been unable to recruit a single litigant here.

The only known public dissent came in a recent sermon by the Rev. William Hess, a Methodist five years in his pulpit here.

But the sermon, in which he held that the Supreme Court was on sound theological as well as constitutional ground in its ruling, brought him "some heat," Mr. Hess said.

The minister has declined the A.C.L.U.'s suggestion that he sue the school board.

"I just don't want to put myself on the block," he said.

Chapter Four

Democratic Representation: One Man - One Vote

Chief Justice Earl Warren, on the occasion of his retirement from the Supreme Court, reviewed the revolutionary era of Constitutional politics over which he presided. The reapportionment cases, he concluded, were the most significant decisions of this era. The importance of those decisions, according to Warren, was momentous.

> If everyone in this country has an opportunity to participate in his government on equal terms with everyone else and can share in electing representatives who will be truly representative of the entire community and not some special interest, then most of these problems that we are now confronted with would be solved through the political process rather than through the courts. (*New York Times*, June 27, 1969.)

Clearly, the series of reapportionment cases beginning with *Baker* v. *Carr* (1962) initiated a new era in representative government.

Because state legislatures had been dominated for years by the rural elements of American society — i.e. farmers, ranchers, "up state" conservatives — most efforts to deal with the urban problems were initiated and supported by the federal government. Self-government becomes most meaningful at the more personal local and state levels of government. Urban voters, being deprived of effective participation at these levels, were disenchanted with republican democracy. *Baker* v. *Carr* provided an opportunity to reverse this trend. Although the revolution in self-government and representation will continue for years to come, it is clear that legislatures may now begin to reflect the needs and desires of the people.

The Fourteenth Amendment reads in part:

> . . . nor shall any State deprive any person of life, liberty, or property, without the due process of law; nor deny to any person within its jurisdiction the equal protection of the laws.

The "equal protection of the laws" clause is the key to the reapportionment revolution. As late as 1946 in *Colegrove* v. *Green*, the Supreme Court denied itself the right to consider the nature and problems of legislative elections. In an exercise of judicial self-restraint the Court ruled that such issues were "non-justiciable." Simply stated, the Court declared that it could not intervene in "political questions" which would bring it into direct conflict with the political branches of government. Reapportionment of state legislatures was, to the Court of 1946, a function of the state legislatures themselves.

Between 1946 and 1962 the demography of America changed drastically. Following the Second World War the growth of urban areas accelerated. This movement to the cities was accompanied with an exodus to suburban regions. However, the states were unable and unwilling to solve problems created by these new urban developments. The city dweller's sole recourse was to the federal government for immediate assistance and to the courts for constitutional redress. Centralized government was an inevitable result. Because of the refusal of state legislatures to reapportion themselves, the Court declared, in 1962, that the 1946 Court had erred—reapportionment was a justiciable issue. Predictably, the reactions to this reversal were clearly political.

Three models have been used to represent the forms representation customarily takes. Most of the political debate surrounding the Court's reapportionment decisions has centered around which form is most appropriate. Although combinations may appear, representation generally takes one of three forms: functional, geographic or popular. Each of these categories has been associated with some form of democracy.

The *functional representation* model assumes that those groups which perform the most meaningful functions in society should be represented in the policy making bodies and that most individuals are associated with at least one such group. Social and economic councils in Europe which advise government and pressure groups in America which are involved in governmental consultation exemplify functional representation.

The numbers of representatives assigned each group will vary according to the importance to the society of the function performed by and the significance of the group. Thus, delegates from the farms, civil service, military, industry, labor, churches, professions etc. would collectively determine state or national policies.

Inherent in functional representation is the notion of elitism. Some groups or people, usually few in number, are considered better able to represent the needs and desires of the total population. What is good for a few of the economic and social leaders of society is good for the society at large. Critics of the Court often argue for functional representation in some form.

The *geographic representation* model, which was more prevalent in America before *Baker v. Carr*, grants to geographical and/or historical areas a specified number of delegates. Counties, states, districts or regions send their delegates to the legislatures. The Senate, representing states (no matter the number of inhabitants), is the best example of such areal representation.

Geographic forms of representation are based on a classical liberal skepticism concerning the uses of power. By granting to geographical units, such as counties, specified degrees of autonomy, these counties will tend to compete and conflict, thus preventing a small group from concentrating and abusing power. A rural county, for example, needs representation equal to that of the urban county, for this prevents the latter from misusing power.

The *popular* model uses population exclusively as the basis for apportioning representation. The one man, one vote principle of the reapportionment decisions accepted popular representation.

Popular representation assumes that whatever the justifications for different forms in government, people are all that count. According to the Supreme Court:

> Legislators represent people, not trees or acres. Legislators are elected by voters, not farms or cities or economic interests. . . . To the extent that a citizen's right to vote is debased, he is that much less a citizen.
> (*Reynolds v. Sims*)

A citizen is not determined by what he does in society, nor by where he lives. If representative government means anything, it means that legislatures represent people and people only. The numbers of delegates to these representative bodies must be in proportion to the number of people those delegates represent.

The Supreme Court has extended the popular form of representation to both houses of state legislatures (*Baker* v. *Carr* and *Reynolds* v. *Sims*), to the House of Representatives at the national level (*Wesberry* v. *Sanders*, 1964), and to local units (*Avery* v. *Midland County*, 1968). At the same time the high court has refused to hear cases involving boards of education and other questionable representative bodies (*Sailors* v. *Bd. of Education of Kent County*, 1967).

Adding to the political controversy in the reapportionment area is that lower courts have been made responsible for enforcing the vague guidelines spelled out by the Supreme Court. And they, in turn, often review lower court decisions. Many states as a consequence have had to face court challenges to their reapportionment plans. The application of one man, one vote has been a continuing political issue, involving state legislatures, who are responsible for redrawing the representative lines; the courts, who review the new plans; and the litigants, usually city dwellers, who are dissatisfied with the results. The continued politics has been exemplified by the Nevada case and the successful challenges to New York State's congressional districts.

Although the Supreme Court has supervised revolutions in a variety of areas, Chief Justice Earl Warren may have been quite correct when he stated that the reapportionment decisions were most crucial and could virtually revitalize representative government in this country.

A "Political Question" Becomes Justiciable (1962)*

Baker v. *Carr*

In the *Baker* case the Court decided that the question of malapportioned state legislatures could be considered within the jurisdiction of the federal courts and that the issue is justiciable. Thus begins the politics of reapportionment. Justice William Brennan delivered the opinion of the Court.

---

*369 U.S. 186.

This civil action was brought to redress the alleged deprivation of federal constitutional rights. The complaint, alleging that by means of a 1901 statute of Tennessee apportioning the members of the General Assembly among the State's 95 counties, "these plaintiffs and others similarly situated, are denied the equal protection of the laws accorded them by the Fourteenth Amendment to the Constitution of the United States by virtue of the debasement of their votes," was dismissed by a three-judge court. We hold that the dismissal was error, and remand the cause to the District Court for trial and further proceedings consistent with this opinion.

The General Assembly of Tennessee consists of the Senate with 33 members and the House of Representatives with 99 members.

Thus, Tennessee's standard for allocating legislative representation among her counties is the total number of qualified voters resident in the respective counties, subject only to minor qualifications. . . . In 1901 the General Assembly abandoned separate enumeration in favor of reliance upon the Federal Census and passed the Apportionment Act here in controversy. In the more than 60 years since that action, all proposals in both Houses of the General Assembly for reapportionment have failed to pass.

Between 1901 and 1961, Tennessee has experienced substantial growth and redistribution of her population. . . . The relative standings of the counties in terms of qualified voters have changed significantly. It is primarily the continued application of the 1901 Apportionment Act to this shifted and enlarged voting population which gives rise to the present controversy. Appellants also argue that, because of the composition of the legislature effected by the 1901 apportionment act, redress in the form of a state constitutional amendment to change the entire mechanism for reapportioning, or any other change short of that, is difficult or impossible. The complaint concludes that "these plaintiffs and others similarly situated, are denied the equal protection of the laws accorded them by the Fourteenth Amendment to the Constitution of the United States by virtue of the debasement of their votes." They seek a declaration that the 1901 statute is unconstitutional and an injunction restraining the appellees from acting to conduct any further elections under it. They also pray that unless and until the General Assembly enacts a valid reapportionment, the District Court should either decree a reapportionment by mathematical application of the Tennessee constitutional formulae to the most recent Federal Census figures, or direct the appellees to conduct legislative elections, primary and general, at large.

. . . .

The District Court was uncertain whether our cases withholding federal judicial relief rested upon a lack of federal jurisdiction or upon the inappropriateness of the subject matter for judicial consideration— what we have designated "nonjusticiability." The distinction between the two grounds is significant. Our conclusion that this cause presents no nonjusticiable "political question" settles the only possible doubt that it is a case or controversy. Under the present heading of "Jurisdiction of the Subject Matter" we hold only that the matter set forth in the complaint does arise under the Constitution. It is clear that the cause of action is one which "arises under" the Federal Constitution. The complaint alleges that the 1901 statute effects an apportionment that deprives the appellants of the equal protection of the laws in violation of the Fourteenth Amendment. Dismissal of the complaint upon the ground of lack of jurisdiction of the subject matter would, therefore, be justified only if that claim were "so attenuated and unsubstantial as to be absolutely devoid of merit." Since the District Court obviously and correctly did not deem the asserted federal constitutional claim unsubstantial and frivolous, it should not have dismissed the complaint for want of jurisdiction of the subject matter.

. . . .

The appellees refer to *Colegrove* v. *Green* . . . as authority that the District Court lacked jurisdiction of the subject matter. Appellees misconceive the holding of that case. The holding was precisely contrary to their reading of it. . . .

We understand the District Court to have read the cited cases as compelling the conclusion that since the appellants sought to have a legislative apportionment held unconstitutional, their suit presented a "political question" and was therefore nonjusticiable. We hold that this challenge to an apportionment presents no nonjusticiable "political question." The cited cases do not hold the contrary.

. . . .

We come, finally to the ultimate inquiry whether our precedents as to what constitutes a nonjusticiable "political question" bring the case before us under the umbrella of that doctrine. A natural beginning is to note whether any of the common characteristics which we have been able to identify and label descriptively are present. We find none: The question here is the consistency of state action with the Federal Constitution. We have no question decided, or to be decided, by a political branch of government coequal with this Court. Nor do we risk embarrassment of our government abroad, or grave disturbance at home if we take issue with Tennessee as to the constitutionality of her action here challenged. Nor need the appellants, in order to succeed in this action, ask the Court to enter upon policy determinations for which judicially manageable standards are lacking. Judicial standards under the Equal Protection Clause are well developed and familiar, and it has been open to courts since the enactment of the Fourteenth Amendment to determine, if on the particular facts they must, that a discrimination reflects no policy, but simply arbitrary and capricious action. . . .

We conclude that the complaint's allegations of a denial of equal protection present a justiciable constitutional cause of action upon which appellants are entitled to a trial and a decision. The right asserted is within the reach of judicial protection under the Fourteenth Amendment.

The judgment of the District Court is reversed and the cause is remanded for further proceedings consistent with this opinion.

Justice Felix Frankfurter, joined by Justice John Harlan, dissented in the following opinion. Note the strong statement of the sources of judicial power in our constitutional system.

The Court today reverses a uniform course of decision established by a dozen cases, including one by which the very claim now sustained was unanimously rejected only five years ago. Such a massive repudiation of the experience of our whole past in asserting destructively novel judicial power demands a detailed analysis of the role of this Court in our constitutional scheme. Disregard of inherent limits in the effective exercise of the Court's "judicial power" not only presages the futility of judicial intervention in the essentially political conflict of forces by which the relation between population and representation has time out of mind been and now is determined. It may well impair the Court's position as the ultimate organ of "the supreme Law of the Land" in that vast range of legal problems, often strongly entangled in popular feeling, on which this Court must pronounce. The Court's authority—possessed neither of the purse nor the sword—ultimately rests on sustained public confidence in its moral sanction. Such feeling must be nourished by the Court's complete detachment, in fact and in appearance, from political entanglements and by abstention from injecting itself into the clash of political forces in political settlements.

. . . .

Justice Harlan, joined by Justice Frankfurter, wrote a dissenting opinion.

The dissenting opinion of Mr. Justice Frankfurter, in which I join, demonstrates the abrupt departure the majority makes from judicial history. . . .

. . . .

I can find nothing in the Equal Protection Clause or elsewhere in the Federal Constitution which expressly or impliedly supports the view that state legislatures must be so structured as to reflect with approximate equality the voice of every voter. Not only is that proposition refuted by history, as shown by my Brother Frankfurter, but it strikes deep into the heart of our federal system. Its acceptance would require us to turn our backs on the regard which this Court has always shown for the judgment of state legislatures and courts on matters of basically local concern.

In the last analysis, what lies at the core of this controversy is a difference of opinion as to the function of representative government.

In short, there is nothing in the Federal Constitution to prevent a State, acting not irrationally, from choosing any electoral legislative structure it thinks best suited to the interests, temper, and customs of its people. . . .

President Kennedy and Reapportionment (1962)*

The Solicitor General under President Kennedy filed a "friend of the court" brief in the *Baker* case arguing for reapportionment. The following excerpts from President Kennedy's news conference indicate the reason for his support of the Court's decision.

Q: Mr. President, would you comment on the Supreme Court reapportionment decision, and say whether there is anything the Federal Government could do to support it?

THE PRESIDENT: I think, as you know, when the matter was before the Supreme Court the administration made clear its endorsement of

---

*Excerpts from President Kennedy's news-conference. John F. Kennedy, *Public Papers of The President of The United States: 1962* (U.S.: Government Printing Office, 1963), pp. 274, 277.

the principles implicit in the Court decision, as a friend of the Court, and I don't think it's probably appropriate to comment on the merits of a specific case in litigation, but I think our position on the general principle was quite clear. Quite obviously, the right to fair representation and to have each vote count equally is, it seems to me, basic to the successful operation of a democracy.

I would hope that through the normal political processes, these changes to insure equality of voting, equality of representation, would be brought about by the responsible groups involved, in the States, and in the National Government.

Now, in the case that was involved here, for many years it was impossible for the people involved to secure adequate relief through the normal political processes. The inequity was built in and therefore there was no chance for a political response to the inequity. The position of the Government, the Federal Government, the administration, as I say, was made clear by Solicitor Cox. And I would hope now the Court having taken a position, I would hope that those responsible in the various States—and this is a matter not confined merely to Tennessee, but it is true of Massachusetts and other States—I would hope that because of the change in population areas that every State would reexamine this problem and attempt to insure equality of voting rights. There's no sense of a Senator's representing 5,000,000 people sitting next to a Senator representing 10,000 people, and then when no relief comes, to say the Court is taking action where it should not. It's the responsibility of the political groups to respond to the need, but if no relief is forthcoming, then of course it would seem to the administration that the judicial branch must meet a responsibility.

· · · · · · · · · · · · · · · · · ·

Q: Mr. President, again on the court decision. It's been suggested that it might be well for the President of the United States to provide some special leadership and direction as a followup to the apportionment decision. How does that strike you?

THE PRESIDENT: Well, I think it's incumbent upon all of those of us who hold office in the States and in the National Government to take every action that we can to have this matter settled by the responsible political groups. And in my earlier statement, I urged these States and State legislatures to carefully reconsider this problem. As I say, those who object to the court taking the action they are taking, it seems to me, are not on very solid ground when they also do not support actions in the States to bring redress. So that I think all of us, in the States, the National Government, the Congress, ought to consider the matter very carefully.

The States vs. Reapportionment (1962)*
Proposed Constitutional Amendments

The following two readings present two reactions to the *Baker* decision. The Council of State Governments, obviously enraged by the Court's ruling, presented the viewpoint of the rurally dominated state legislatures. Not only did they wish to take reapportionment out of the hands of the Supreme Court, but the states wished to establish a Court of the Union which would supervise Supreme Court decisions. The American Bar Association on the other hand for a variety of reasons rejects the Council's constitutional amendments.

Article V of the United States Constitution should be amended to read as follows:

Section 1. The Congress, whenever two-thirds of both Houses shall deem it necessary, or, on the application of the Legislatures of two-thirds of the several States, shall propose amendments to this Constitution which shall be valid to all intents and purposes, as part of this Constitution, when ratified by the Legislatures of three-fourths of the several States. Whenever applications from the Legislatures of two-thirds of the total number of States of the United States shall contain identical texts of an amendment to be proposed, the President of the Senate and the Speaker of the House of Representatives shall so certify, and the amendment as contained in the application shall be deemed to have been proposed without further action by Congress. . . .

It was proposed that this provision be added to the Constitution:

Section 1. No provision of this Constitution, or any amendment thereto, shall restrict or limit any state in the apportionment of representation in its legislature.

---

*Proposed by the General Assembly of the Council of State Governments. *Congressional Record* (Feb. 14, 1963), p. 13035.

Section 2. The judicial power of the United States shall not extend to any suit in law or equity, or to any controversy, relating to apportionment of representation in a state legislature. . . .

This amendment to the Constitution was proposed:

Article—

Section 1. Upon demand of the legislatures of five states, no two of which shall share any common boundary, made within two years after the rendition of any judgment of the Supreme Court relating to the rights reserved to the states or to the people by this Constitution, such judgment shall be reviewed by a Court composed of the chief justices of the highest courts of the several states to be known as the Court of the Union. The sole issue before the Court of the Union shall be whether the power or jurisdiction sought to be exercised on the part of the United States is a power granted to it under this Constitution.

Section 2. Three-fourths of the justices of the Court of the Union shall constitute a quorum, but it shall require concurrence of a majority of the entire Court to reverse a decision of the Supreme Court.

.   .   .   .

Section 4. Decisions of the Court of the Union upon matters within its jurisdiction shall be final and shall not thereafter be overruled by any court and may be changed only by an amendment of this Constitution.

.   .   .   .

The Bar and Critics Of The Court (1963)*
House Of Delegates of the American Bar Association

Mr. W— then introduced his first resolution, which affirmed the stand taken by the Board of Governors in May.

Resolved, That the American Bar Association disapproves and opposes the proposal of the Council of State Governments, the terms of which would create a fifty justice Court of the Union.

Mr. W— said that it was the view of his Committee that the Court-of-the-Union proposal was unsound and inimical to the federal

---

*Reprinted with permission from the *American Bar Association Journal*, October, 1963, pp. 986–987.

system. "It is divisive; it is impractical; it is unwieldly; it is undesirable," he declared.

.   .   .   .

The resolution was then approved in the form it appears above. Mr. W— then offered a resolution which would have placed the Association on record as favoring the apportionment proposal of the Council of State Governments. The majority of the Committee had felt that there has been a growing imbalance in the federal-state relationship, he explained, and this proposal would draw a line against further broadening of federal power. The final arbiter of the state's representation in its own legislature should be the state's own supreme court, not the Supreme Court of the United States, he went on, and if the federal judiciary can order recomposition of state legislatures, it can run and control the machinery of state government. Further, if a federal court is to reapportion a legislature, he asked, "What is to be the standard? What is to be the formula? . . . Is it to be geography, economics, special interests? There is no rational or reasonable end to this road of federal interference with state affairs."

Mr. S—, in opposition to the Committee's resolution, argued that there was no standard set forth in the Council of State Governments' proposed amendment and if it were adopted it would mean that a legislature might set any standards, any limitation or discrimination it chose. That would return us to a confederacy, he said. *Baker* v. *Carr* is the result of the fact that the State of Tennessee did not comply with its own Constitution, he declared. What the Court held, in effect, was "If there is a rational policy or even taxation perhaps . . . it may be good if applied properly," Mr. S— asserted. He moved to amend the resolution of the Committee by deleting the word "approves" and substituting "disapproves and opposes."

Mr. M— of Louisiana, speaking in favor of the Committee's resolution and against Mr. S— amendment, said that if the Federal Government has the authority to reapportion the legislature of a state, by the same reasoning it has jurisdiction to reapportion all the other agencies of the state, including boards of county commissioners, police juries, city councils and school boards. He conceded that there were inequities in apportionment because of shifts in population, but he declared that the elimination of these was a matter for the states.

Mr. F— of Oklahoma City said that the hard fact was that the people of many states had not been able to obtain representation in accordance with the guarantees of their own state constitutions. "We haven't got any place to go except to the federal courts, under the

Federal Constitution," he said. He declared that if the Council of State Governments' proposal were adopted it would be "the first diminution in American history of any federal constitutional guarantee of liberty, of justice or equality."

Mr. R— of Salt Lake City declared that *Baker* v. *Carr* was a "door-opener" to further extension of the power of the federal judiciary. "Does *Baker* v. *Carr* represent a philosophy that is dangerous to the destruction of the federal form of government and the destruction of the states?" he asked. "Certainly this amendment (proposed by the Council of State Governments) simply reaffirms the doctrine of the Tenth Amendment," he declared.

. . . .

Mr. W— summing up for the Committee, said that the effect of *Baker* v. *Carr* was to give nine men the authority to run the legislatures of the fifty states and the Committee believed that this was contrary to the Tenth Amendment. The proper place for citizens to go to obtain redress of redistricting grievances was the supreme court of their own state, he continued, and the Committee's resolution "would tend to draw a line which needs to be drawn against an all-powerful, all-pervasive, centralized national government." . . .

. . . .

Mr. R— said that the real issue was the right to vote. The Fourteenth Amendment guarantees the right to vote, he continued, and under it the states cannot grant one man twenty votes, another a thousand votes, and someone else only one vote. All that *Baker* v. *Carr* held, he said, was that the courts must enforce the equal protection provisions of the Fourteenth Amendment.

. . . .

The House then adopted the resolution as amended, which read as follows: . . .

Resolved, That the American Bar Association disapproves and opposes the proposal of the Council of State Governments proposing an amendment to the Constitution of the United States providing that no provision of the Constitution shall restrict or limit any state in the apportionment of representation in its legislature and that the judicial power of the United States shall not extend to any suit in law or equity, or to any controversy relating to apportionment of representation in a state legislature.

Mr. W— then moved adoption of the Committee's third resolution, which affirmed the position taken by the Board of Governors in opposition to the Council of State Governments' suggested change in the amending process. The resolution, . . .

Resolved, That the American Bar Association disapproves and opposes the proposal of the Council of State Governments proposing a constitutional amendment to Article V by the terms of which state legislatures would be empowered to initiate and ratify a constitutional amendment without action by the Congress of the United States.

. . . .

The House then voted to adopt the Committee's resolution.

The "Federal Analogy" (1964)*

Reynolds v. Sims

One man, one vote is a principle which applies to upper houses of state legislatures as well as lower houses. In the following case the Justices reject the federal analogy—that states should have an upper house based on area—and thereby justifying their ruling. Chief Justice Earl Warren delivered the opinion of the Court.

... [T]he right of suffrage is a fundamental matter in a free and democratic society. Especially since the right to exercise the franchise in a free and unimpaired manner is preservative of other basic civil and political rights, any alleged infringement of the right of citizens to vote must be carefully and meticulously scrutinized. . . .

Legislators represent people, not trees or acres. Legislators are elected by voters, not farms or cities or economic interests. As long as ours is a representative form of government, and our legislatures are those instruments of government elected directly by and directly representative of the people, the right to elect legislators in a free and unimpaired fashion is a bedrock of our political system. . . . Overweighting and overvaluation of the votes of those living here has the certain effect of dilution and undervaluation of the votes of those living there. The resulting discrimination against those individual voters living in disfavored areas is easily demonstrable mathematically. Their right to vote is simply not the same right to vote as that of those living in a favored part of the State. . . .

---

*377 U.S. 533.

State legislatures are, historically, the fountainhead of representative government in this country.... With the birth of our National
Government, and the adoption and ratification of the Federal Constitution, state legislatures retained a most important place in our
Nation's governmental structure. But representative government is in
essence self-government through the medium of elected representatives
of the people, and each and every citizen has an inalienable right to
full and effective participation in the political processes of his State's
legislative bodies. Most citizens can achieve this participation only as
qualified voters through the election of legislators to represent them.
Full and effective participation by all citizens in state government
requires, therefore, that each citizen has an equally effective voice
in the election of members of his state legislature. Modern and viable
state government needs, and the Constitution demands, no less.

Logically, in a society ostensibly grounded on representative government, it would seem reasonable that a majority of the people of a
State could elect a majority of that State's legislators. To conclude
differently, and to sanction minority control of state legislative bodies,
would appear to deny majority rights in a way that far surpasses any
possible denial of minority rights that might otherwise be thought to
result. . . . Our constitutional system amply provides for the protection
of minorities by means other than giving them majority control of
state legislatures.

. . . .

To the extent that a citizen's right to vote is debased, he is that
much less a citizen. The fact that an individual lives here or there is
not a legitimate reason for overweighting or diluting the efficacy of
his vote. The complexions of societies and civilizations change, often
with amazing rapidity. A nation once primarily rural in character
becomes predominantly urban. Representation schemes once fair and
equitable become archaic and outdated. But the basic principle of
representative government remains, and must remain, unchanged—
the weight of a citizen's vote cannot be made to depend on where he
lives. . . .

We hold that, as a basic constitutional standard, the Equal Protection Clause requires that the seats in both houses of a bicameral
state legislature must be apportioned on a population basis. Simply
stated, an individual's right to vote for state legislators is unconstitutionally impaired when its weight is in a substantial fashion diluted
when compared with votes of citizens living in other parts of the State.

. . . .

Much has been written since our decision in *Baker* v. *Carr* about the applicability of the so-called federal analogy to state legislative apportionment arrangements. . . . We agree with the District Court, and find the federal analogy inapposite and irrelevant to state legislative districting schemes. Attempted reliance on the federal analogy appears often to be little more than an after-the-fact rationalization offered in defense of maladjusted state apportionment arrangements. . . .

The system of representation in the two Houses of the Federal Congress is one ingrained in our Constitution, as part of the law of the land. It is one conceived out of compromise and concession indispensable to the establishment of our federal republic. Arising from unique historical circumstances, it is based on the consideration that in establishing our type of federalism a group of formerly independent States bound themselves together under one national government. . . .

Political subdivisions of States—counties, cities, or whatever— never were and never have been considered as sovereign entities. Rather, they have been traditionally regarded as subordinate governmental instrumentalities created by the State to assist in the carrying out of state governmental functions. . . .

. . . .

Since we find the so-called federal analogy inapposite to a consideration of the constitutional validity of state legislative apportionment schemes, we necessarily hold that the Equal Protection Clause requires both houses of a state legislature to be apportioned on a population basis. The right of a citizen to equal representation and to have his vote weighted equally with those of all other citizens in the election of members of one house of a bicameral state legislature would amount to little if States could effectively submerge the equal-population principle in the apportionment of seats in the other house.

. . . .

By holding that as a federal constitutional requisite both houses of a state legislature must be apportioned on a population basis, we mean that the Equal Protection Clause requires that a State make an honest and good faith effort to construct districts, in both houses of its legislature, as nearly of equal population as is practicable. We realize that it is a practical impossibility to arrange legislative districts so that each one has an identical number of residents, or citizens, or voters. Mathematical exactness or precision is hardly a workable constitutional requirement.

. . . .

Whatever the means of accomplishment, the overriding objective must be substantial equality of population among the various districts, so that the vote of any citizen is approximately equal in weight to that of any other citizen in the State.

. . . .

Justice Tom Clark wrote a separate concurring opinion. In a brief separate opinion Justice Potter Stewart also voted to affirm the judgment of the District Court. Justice John Harlan dissented as follows.

Today's holding is that the Equal Protection Clause of the Fourteenth Amendment requires every State to structure its legislature so that all the members of each house represent substantially the same number of people; other factors may be given play only to the extent that they do not significantly encroach on this basic "population" principle. Whatever may be thought of this holding as a piece of political ideology—and even on that score the political history and practices of this country from its earliest beginnings leave wide room for debate. . . . I think it demonstrable that the Fourteenth Amendment does not impose this political tenet on the States or authorize this Court to do so. . . .

. . . .

[This decision] also cut[s] deeply into the fabric of our federalism. What must follow . . . may eventually appear to be the product of State Legislatures. Nevertheless, no thinking person can fail to recognize that the aftermath of these cases, however desirable it may be thought in itself, will have been achieved at the cost of a radical alteration in the relationship between the States and the Federal Government, more particularly the Federal Judiciary. Only one who has an overbearing impatience with the federal system and its political processes will believe that that cost was not too high or was inevitable.

The Dirksen Amendment (1965)*

Although the following proposed constitutional amendment was defeated by Congress, Senator Dirksen had, by July, 1969, succeeded in gaining all but one of the required state legislative resolutions calling

*Congressional Record, August 11, 1965, p. 19375.

for a constitutional convention. Presumably this convention would be limited to proposing to the states some form of the Dirksen Amendment.

That the following article is proposed as an amendment to the Constitution of the United States. . . .

Section 1. The legislature of each state shall be apportioned by the people of that state at each general election for Representatives to the Congress held next following the year in which there is commenced each enumeration provided for in Section 2 of Article I. In the case of a bicameral legislature, the members of one house shall be apportioned among the people on the basis of their numbers and the members of the other house may be apportioned among the people on the basis of population, geography, and political subdivisions in order to insure effective representation in the state's legislature of the various groups and interests making up the electorate. In the case of a unicameral legislature, the house may be apportioned among the people on the basis of substantial equality of population with such weight given to geography and political subdivisions as will insure effective representation in the state's legislature of the various groups and interests making up the electorate.

Section 2. A plan of apportionment shall become effective only after it has been submitted to a vote of the people of the state and approved by a majority of those voting on that issue at a statewide election held in accordance with law and the provisions of this Constitution.

.   .   .   .

A Lower Court Applies Reapportionment Guidelines (1966)*

As in the desegregation cases, the Supreme Court turned over the application of its reapportionment decisions to lower federal courts. In the following case the legislative reapportionment plan for the Nevada State Assembly and Senate was challenged. The Federal District Court for Nevada, after reviewing the guidelines of the Supreme

---

Dungan v. *Sawyer*, March 21, 1966. The opinion was signed by Stanley N. Barnes, U.S. Circuit Judge; Roger D. Foley, U.S. District Judge and Bruce R. Thompson, U.S. District Judge.

Court and other courts, ruled in favor of the legislature. This same legislative–judicial process in applying the reapportionment decisions was being utilized throughout the United States.

In its opinion filed September 23, 1965, . . . this Court held that certain provisions of Nevada's constitution and statutes pertaining to legislative apportionment violated the equal protective clause of the Fourteenth Amendment of the Constitution of the United States and were invidiously discriminatory, being based upon no constitutionally valid policy. The Court ordered the Governor of Nevada to convene a special session of the Legislature for the sole purpose of constitutionally apportioning the Senate and Assembly.

In special session, the Legislature passed, and the Governor approved, Chapter 2, Statutes of Nevada, 1965 Special Session, to become effective June 1, 1966, if approved by this Court.

. . . . The Plaintiffs . . . urge the Court to reject Chapter 2, contending that this reapportionment plan does not meet the test set forth in *Reynolds* v. *Sims*, . . . in that the population of the districts created by the Act are not as equal as practicable.

The general principles that must guide us in determining whether or not Chapter 2 is constitutionally permissive are to be found in six cases decided by the Supreme Court in June of 1964. . . .

We adopt, in part, from *Honsey* v. *Donovan* (Minn., 1964, 236 F. Supp. 8) that court's summary of pertinent points of law:

1. The equal protection clause of the Fourteenth Amendment requires substantially equal legislative representation for all citizens of a state. This is the basic concept.

2. "The Equal Protection Clause requires that a State make an honest and good faith effort to construct districts, in both houses of its legislature, as nearly of equal population as is practicable." . . .

3. But "Mathematical exactness or precision is hardly a workable constitutional requirement." . . . Rather, the proper judicial approach, is to ascertain whether . . . there has been a faithful adherence to a plan of population-based representation, with such minor deviations only as may occur in recognizing certain factors that are free from any taint of arbitrariness or discrimination." . . .

4. "So long as the divergences from a strict population standard are based on legitimate considerations incident to the effectuation of a rational state policy, some deviations from the equal-population principle are constitutionally permissible. . . ."

5. However, weighting of votes according to area is discriminatory. A "built-in bias against voters living in the State's more populous counties" does not meet constitutional standards. . . . Also, "neither

history alone, nor economic or other sorts of group interests, are permissible factors in attempting to justify disparities from population-based representation. Citizens, not history or economic interests, cast votes." . . .

6. A state "can rationally consider according political subdivisions some independent representation in at least one body of the state legislature, as long as the basic standard of equality of population among districts is maintained" and "provide for compact districts of contiguous territory." . . .

7. "It is simply impossible to decide upon the validity of the apportionment of one house of a bicameral legislature in the abstract, without also evaluating the actual scheme of representation employed with respect to the other house." . . .

8. Reapportionment "is primarily a matter for legislative consideration and determination, and . . . judicial relief becomes appropriate only when a legislature fails to reapportion according to federal constitutional requisites in a timely fashion after having had an adequate opportunity to do so." . . .

. . . .

Within the guidelines laid down by the Supreme Court, a number of three-judge district courts and state supreme courts have considered three tests as major factors in evaluating state legislative apportionment schemes:

(a) Calculate the population ratio between districts having the largest and the smallest population per representative for each house of the legislature (referred to herein as the maximum population variance ratio);

(b) Determine the minimum percentage of persons in the state who elect a majority in each house of the legislature;

(c) Calculate the percentage of deviation from the result obtained by dividing the population of the state by the number of seats in each house of the legislature.

. . . .

Nevada's population in 1960 was 285,278 persons. Approximately 75% of the population resided in two counties, approximately 45% in Clark County (Las Vegas) and 30% in Washoe County (Reno).

Senate

Under Chapter 2, the Nevada State Senate will be composed of 20 senators elected from 13 districts. Based upon a 1960 population of 285,278, the average district would have 14,264 persons per senator.

The population per senator ranges from 11,240 for the least populous district to 16,558 for the most populous district. The maximum population variance ratio is 1 to 1.47. The greatest variation from the average is 21.2%, and 49.7% of the population is required to elect a majority, or 11 senators.

Stated another way, 6 districts (14 of the least populous counties, exclusive of Storey County), having a combined population of 72,951, elect 6 senators, 1 for each 12,159 persons. Compared with the ideal or average of 14,264, these 6 districts are 14.7% below the average, and thus they are over-represented by 14.7%.

Three districts (Washoe and Storey Counties), having a combined population of 85,311 (Storey is the least populous county, the 1960 population being only 568 persons) elect 6 senators, or 1 for each 14,219 persons. These 3 districts are .31% under average. This is very close to the ideal or average of 14,264.

Four districts (Clark County), having a population of 127,016, elect 8 senators, or 1 senator for each 15,877 persons. This is 11.3% over the average; hence, these 4 districts are under-represented by 11.3%.

Assembly

Chapter 2 provides for 16 assembly districts electing 40 assemblymen. The average or ideal population per assemblyman is 7,132 persons. The population per assemblyman ranges from 5,532 for the least populous district to 8,452 persons for the most populous district. The maximum population variance ratio is 1 to 1.53. The greatest variation from the average is 22.4%, and 46.8% of the population is required to elect a majority of the assembly.

Stated otherwise, 9 districts (14 of the least populous counties, exclusive of Storey County), with a combined population of 72,951, elect 12 assemblymen, 1 for each 6,079 persons, compared with an average or ideal of 7,132. These 9 districts are 14.7% under average, and thus are over-represented by 14.7%.

Two districts (Washoe and Storey Counties), having a combined population of 85,311, elect 12 assemblymen, or 1 assemblyman for each 7,109 persons. This is a variance of .32% from the average. This is very close to the ideal or average.

Five districts (Clark County), having a population of 127,016 persons, elect 16 assemblymen, or 1 for each 7,938 persons. This is 11% over the average and hence these 5 districts are under-represented by 11%.

.   .   .   .

Conclusion

Chapter 2 is not the fairest and best plan that the Nevada Legislature could possibly enact. Unquestionably, the Legislature could be reapportioned in a manner so that the population of each district electing senators and assemblymen could be much closer to the average or ideal. . . . However, this Court may not reject Chapter 2 simply because it believes more equally population-based plans are possible or practicable. What we must decide, here, is whether or not, after considering all of the circumstances existing in Nevada pertinent to legislative apportionment, Chapter 2, viewed as a whole, is constitutionally permissive. If the variation from the average or ideally population-based representation is within permissible limits, we must approve even though there may be other apportionment schemes that would be more nearly population based.

. . . .

Viewed as a whole, Chapter 2 is a population-based plan of representation, and this Court cannot say that the deviations from a strict population standard are not based upon legitimate considerations in carrying out rational state policy and this Court cannot say that the plan is tainted with arbitrariness or discrimination or that there is a built-in bias against voters living in the State's most populous counties. We therefore approve Chapter 2, Statutes of Nevada, 1965 Special Session.

The Court Continues Supervision of Reapportionment (1969)*

Wells v. Rockefeller

In *Wesberry v. Sanders* (1964) the Supreme Court applied the one man, one vote principle to the House of Representatives. Five years later, in a decision by Justice William Brennan, the Court overruled a lower court's decision and invalidated a reapportionment scheme devised by the New York State legislature.

. . . .

---

*89 S. Ct. 1234.

The heart of the districting scheme, lay in the decision to treat seven sections of the State as homogeneous regions and to divide each region into congressional districts of virtually identical population. Thirty-one of New York's 41 congressional districts were constructed on that principle. The remaining 10 districts were composed of groupings of whole counties. . . .

It is clear that our decision in *Kirkpatrick* v. *Preisler*, compels the conclusion that this scheme is unconstitutional. We there held, that "the command of Art. 1, § 2, that States create congressional districts which provide equal representation for equal numbers of people permits only the limited population variances which are unavoidable despite a good-faith effort to achieve absolute equality, or for which justification is shown." The general command, of course, is to equalize population in all the districts of the State and is not satisfied by equalizing population only within defined sub-states. New York could not and does not claim that the legislature made a good-faith effort to achieve precise mathematical equality among its 41 congressional districts. Rather, New York tries to justify its scheme of constructing equal districts only within each of seven sub-states as a means to keep regions with distinct interests intact. But we made clear in *Kirkpatrick* that "to accept population variances, large or small, in order to create districts with specific interest orientations is antithetical to the basic premise of the constitutional command to provide equal representation for equal numbers of people." To accept a scheme such as New York's would permit groups of districts with defined interest orientations to be over-represented at the expense of districts with different interest orientations. Equality of population among districts in a sub-state is not a justification for inequality among all the districts in the state.

Nor are the variations in the "North country" districts justified by the fact that these districts are constructed of entire counties.

We appreciate that the decision of the District Court did not rest entirely on an appraisal of the merits of the New York plan. As noted earlier, when the three-judge District Court in 1967 held the then-existing districting plan unconstitutional, it recognized that the imminence of the 1968 election made re-districting an unrealistic possibility and therefore said only that "there are enough changes which can be super-imposed on the present districts to cure the most flagrant inequalities." 273 F. Supp., at 992. . . .

On February 26, 1968, the New York Legislature enacted the plan before us. On March 20, 1968, the District Court approved the plan for both the 1968 and 1970 congressional elections. Since the 1968 primary election was only three months away on March 20, we cannot say that there was error in permitting the 1968 election to proceed under the plan despite its constitutional infirmities. . . .

But ample time remains to promulgate a plan meeting constitutional standards before the election machinery must be set in motion for the 1970 election. . . .

Justice Abe Fortas concurred and Justices John Harlan, Potter Stewart, and Byron White dissented.

Chapter Five

Freedom of Expression: Pornography and the Law

The First Amendment to the U.S. Constitution prevents Congress from enacting laws which abridge "the freedom of speech or of the press." The basic assumption is that freedom of expression is essential to the workings of a democracy; therefore, even opinions which are repugnant to the majority must be protected. Unfortunately, a line has traditionally been drawn between protected speech and writings and expression which falls outside the protection of the First Amendment. Two areas of expression have fallen within this latter category: pornography and seditious or "fighting" words. Pornography presents most of the problems inherent in the area of free speech.

Nineteenth century America provided a simple answer to the issue of pornography. Novels and art had to have a moral purpose. Books had to be in good taste and refined. Victorian conscience ruled America's morals. In 1865, Congress banned from the mails anything too "indelicate for family use." Judgment by the courts as to what was to be tolerated relied on the *Hicklin* test, which English courts had enunciated in 1868. Material was obscene and therefore not protected according to the *Hicklin* test if,

> . . . the tendency of the matter charged . . . is to deprave and corrupt
> those whose minds are open to such immoral influences and into whose
> hands a publication of this sort may fall.

In effect, this meant freedom of expression in the area of pornography extended only to that which was safe for children.

In America Anthony Comstock ruled over what would be acceptable reading for the public. Pornography, for Anthony Comstock,

> breeds lust. Lust defiles the body, debauches the imagination, corrupts the mind, deadens the will, destroys the memory, sears the conscience, hardens the heart and damns the soul.

In 1873 Congress enacted the "Comstock Act" which prevented the use of the U.S. Mails for "indecent" material. Comstock bragged that he personally had destroyed fifty tons of indecent books, 28,425 lbs. of printing plates and nearly four million obscene pictures.

Although the lower courts began to question the desirability of the *Hicklin* test, the twentieth century saw no significant constitutional changes by the Supreme Court until *Roth* v. *U.S.* in 1957. Prior to this landmark case, federal, state and local courts and legislatures, often with contradictory results, supervised what Americans could read and view. The Supreme Court simply avoided the issue.

In the *Roth* decision of 1957, the Justices defined obscene material as

> material which deals with sex in a manner appealing to prurient interest, and the test of obscenity is whether the average person, applying contemporary standards, the dominant theme of the material taken as a whole appeals to prurient interests.

Although the test seemed to satisfy the demands of both those advocating some freedom and those who would supervise our morals, the Supreme Court was brought under pressure simply because its *Roth* test appeared to prevent local control over artistic dissent. Local, state and federal legislation had now to comply with the *Roth* standard.

Nine years later, in the *Fanny Hill* case, the Justices shocked their critics by redirecting the *Roth* test and making "redeeming social value" the paramount standard for defining obscenity. If a book had any redeeming social value, however slight, it was protected by the First Amendment. The same day the Court added another confusing dimension to the obscenity issue. Even though the literature under question may not be obscene itself, the manner in which it was sold could be taken into account to determine if its predominant appeal was to prurient interests. (*Ginzburg* v. *U.S.* 1966.) Nonetheless, the *Ginzburg* decision failed to placate those who saw the Supreme Court as the institution opening the door for disgusting and harmful forms of art.

In 1968 the high court upheld a state law which made it a crime to sell certain materials to minors (*Ginzburg* v. *N.Y.*). Clean literature advocates were encouraged. However, a year later the Justices extended the scope of the First Amendment protections to private uses of pornography. In *Stanley* v. *Georgia*, the Court ruled that pornographic materials kept by an individual for use in his own home were protected. As in the two 1966 cases the Court broadened the scope of freedom of expression and at the same time appeared to submit to pressure by upholding state laws which were designed to control sale of pornography to minors.

Three approaches to pornography and the law have been involved in the politics concerning obscenity. The *restrictive* approach was adopted by the majority of Americans during the Comstock era. The *moderate* school of thought constitutes the law and politics of pornography today. The *permissive* approach has been advocated by some and appears to be gaining further advocates.

The *restrictive school* attaches a value to forms of moral behavior in and of themselves. Morals are absolutes. For example, marriage is good; any threat to it is bad. Because those who produce pornography may debase marriage, they are not to be tolerated. The restrictive approach assumes that morals are truths which do not change. Finally, advocates of this approach assume that some individuals can and must act as censor to protect the public. Freedom of expression and especially pornographic forms of expression shall be closely supervised.

The *moderate approach* claims that a shared morality is the cement of society. Without a consensus on moral values, society would not exist. Although no harm may come directly to others, certain immoral practices encouraged by pornography may ultimately destroy society. For example, marriage and the family are basic social institutions. Adultery, homosexuality, promiscuity—presumably encouraged by pornographic art and literature—would be destructive of marriage and the family. Therefore, the law must control pornography. The moderates assume first that sexual morality is directly related to other practices antithetical to society such as robbery, killing, violence, subversion, delinquency, etc. Second, the morality which holds society together is a seamless web. A break in one thread will soon lead to the disintegration of the total fabric.

The *permissive approach* is best exemplified on the Supreme Court by Justices Black and Douglas. In *Roth*, Douglas wrote that he would "give the broad sweep of the First Amendment full support" in the area of pornography.

> I have the same confidence in the ability of our people to reject noxious literature as I have in their capacity to sort out the true from the false in theology, economics, politics and any other field.

The only purpose of laws controlling extreme forms of dissent would be to protect others from harm. Underlying this approach is the assumption that man is reasonable. Ultimately, a reasonable man will arrive at the best guides for behavior if exposed to any and all forms of expression.

Each approach is illustrated in the selections which follow. As the Court took a position on the permissive wing of the moderate approach, Congress—followed by the President and state legislatures joined the battle. Those guardians of American morals—the Churches—agreed that the flood of obscenity on the newsstands constituted a greater threat to them than did the banning of religious readings in school. Many have led to the attack on the Court.

The issue of obscenity and the law is clearly far from settled. For one thing, many of the leading decisions have been 5–4 rulings. The political pressures may cause shifts by individual Justices. Also, the fact that many of the Court's rulings in this area are vague will necessitate continuing review, possibly allowing a later Court to withdraw sufficiently to allow the people to decide through local laws. But the fortress of the First Amendment is truly formidable.

"Obscenity is Not Protected Speech" (1957)*

Roth v. *United States*

The *Roth* case is the first time the Supreme Court faced the issue of pornography and the First Amendment. Prior to the 1957 decision, state and local laws generally regulated rather restrictively the distribution of pornographic materials. Justice William Brennan delivered the opinion of the Court.

. . . .

The dispositive question is whether obscenity is utterance within the area of protected speech and press. Although this is the first time the question has been squarely presented to this Court, either under the First Amendment or under the Fourteenth Amendment, expressions found in numerous opinions indicate that this Court has always as-

*354 U.S. 476.

sumed that obscenity is not protected by the freedoms of speech and press. . . .

. . . .

All ideas having even the slightest redeeming social importance—unorthodox ideas, controversial ideas, even ideas hateful to the prevailing climate of opinion—have the full protection of the guaranties, unless excludable because they encroach upon the limited area of more important interests. But implicit in the history of the First Amendment is the rejection of obscenity as utterly without redeeming social impcrtance. This rejection for that reason is mirrored in the universal judgment that obscenity should be restrained, reflected in the international agreement of over 50 nations, in the obscenity laws of all of the 48 States, and in the 20 obscenity laws enacted by the Congress from 1842 to 1956. . . . We hold that obscenity is not within the area of constitutionally protected speech or press.

It is strenuously urged that these obscenity statutes offend the constitutional guaranties because they punish incitation to impure sexual thoughts, not shown to be related to any overt antisocial conduct which is or may be incited in the persons stimulated to such thoughts. . . . It is insisted that the constitutional guaranties are violated because convictions may be had without proof either that obscene material will perceptibly create a clear and present danger of antisocial conduct, or will probably induce its recipients to such conduct. But, in light of our holding that obscenity is not protected speech, the complete answer to this argument is in the holding of this Court in *Beauharnais* v. *Illinois*, . . . :

> Libelous utterances not being within the area of constitutionally protected speech, it is unnecessary, either for us or for the State courts, to consider the issues behind the phrase "clear and present danger." Certainly no one would contend that obscene speech, for example, may be punished only upon a showing of such circumstances. Libel, as we have seen, is in the same class.

However, sex and obscenity are not synonymous. Obscene material is material which deals with sex in a manner appealing to prurient interest. The portrayal of sex, e. g., in art, literature and scientific works, is not itself sufficient reason to deny material the constitutional protection of freedom of speech and press. Sex, a great and mysterious motive force in human life, has indisputably been a subject of absorbing interest to mankind through the ages; it is one of the vital problems of human interest and public concern. . . .

The fundamental freedoms of speech and press have contributed greatly to the development and well-being of our free society and are indispensable to its continued growth. Ceaseless vigilance is the watchword to prevent their erosion by Congress or by the States. The door barring federal and state intrusion into this area cannot be left ajar; it must be kept tightly closed and opened only the slightest crack necessary to prevent encroachment upon more important interests. It is therefore vital that the standards for judging obscenity safeguard the protection of freedom of speech and press for material which does not treat sex in a manner appealing to prurient interest.

The early leading standard of obscenity allowed material to be judged merely by the effect of an isolated excerpt upon particularly susceptible persons. . . . Some American courts adopted this standard but later decisions have rejected it and substituted this test: whether to the average person, applying contemporary community standards, the dominant theme of the material taken as a whole appeals to prurient interest. The Hicklin test, judging obscenity by the effect of isolated passages upon the most susceptible persons, might well encompass material legitimately treating with sex, and so it must be rejected as unconstitutionally restrictive of the freedoms of speech and press. On the other hand, the substituted standard provides safeguards adequate to withstand the charge of constitutional infirmity.

. . . .

Justice John Harlan dissented.

. . . . Every communication has an individuality and "value" of its own. The suppression of a particular writing or other tangible form of expression is, therefore, an individual matter, and in the nature of things every such suppression raises an individual constitutional problem, in which a reviewing court must determine for itself whether the attacked expression is suppressible within constitutional standards. Since those standards do not readily lend themselves to generalized definitions, the constitutional problem in the last analysis becomes one of particularized judgments which appellate courts must make for themselves.

I do not think that reviewing courts can escape this responsibility by saying that the trier of the facts, be it a jury or a judge, has labeled the questioned matter as "obscene," for, if "obscenity" is to be suppressed, the question whether a particular work is of that character involves not really an issue of fact but a question of constitutional judgment of the most sensitive and delicate kind. . . . In short, I do not understand how the Court can resolve the constitutional problems now before it without making its own independent judgment upon the character of the material upon which these convictions were based. . . .

. . . .

Justice William Douglas, with whom Justice Hugo Black concurred, dissented as follows.

When we sustain these convictions, we make the legality of a publication turn on the purity of thought which a book or tract instills in the mind of the reader. I do not think we can approve that standard and be faithful to the command of the First Amendment, which by its terms is a restraint on Congress and which by the Fourteenth is a restraint on the States.

. . . .

By these standards punishment is inflicted for thoughts provoked, not for overt acts nor antisocial conduct. This test cannot be squared with our decisions under the First Amendment. . . .

. . . .

Freedom of expression can be suppressed if, and to the extent that, it is so closely brigaded with illegal action as to be an inseparable part of it. . . . As a people, we cannot afford to relax that standard. For the test that suppresses a cheap tract today can suppress a literary gem tomorrow. All it need do is to incite a lascivious thought or arouse a lustful desire. The list of books that judges or juries can place in that category is endless.

I would give the broad sweep of the First Amendment full support. I have the same confidence in the ability of our people to reject noxious literature as I have in their capacity to sort out the true from the false in theology, economics, politics, or any other field.

Obscenity and Censorship (1960)*

According to many the problem of obscenity in American literature and arts can be handled in a far more satisfactory manner than through the law and police or through self-styled clean literature committees. The following article suggests alternative methods.

The emotional tensions that surround any discussion of sexual mores, and perhaps particularly any discussion of written or pictorial

---

*Dan Lacy, "Obscenity and Censorship," *Christian Century*, May 4, 1960, pp. 540–543. Copyright 1960 Christian Century Foundation. Reprinted with permission of publishers.

representations of sex, are so great that any objective inquiry into the problem is quite difficult. For some reason it is much easier to take a dispassionate view of murder or kidnaping or atomic destruction than of "obscenity." But let us try.

What are the facts? Is there a sudden new outpouring of material creating a moral crisis? When people speak of [a] . . . "pagan flood," they may have one or more of four rather distinct kinds of material in mind. One is "hard-core" pornography: usually photographs or motion pictures of persons engaged in sexual and perverted acts and written material of comparable character. These materials are never sold openly but peddled or shown surreptitiously with no pretense of legality. Prices are usually quite high, and the market probably consists very largely of adults of perverted taste who collect such material. It is rarely if ever seen by most persons.

The second general type of material is openly sold or exhibited and endeavors to stay within, but just within, the law. It is entirely commercially motivated and has no other purpose than the exploitation of sex. This type of material is most notably represented today by "girlie" magazines consisting of partially nude or nude photographs and formula-written stories of sex and by "burlesque" films shown at certain theaters. It is this type which at present most vividly attracts the censors' attentions.

The third general category consists of novels, plays or motion pictures of a general character, making up part of the regular flow of publication or of film distribution through normal channels. These are likely to speak of sexual matters with greater candor and to report conversations with greater fidelity than was permissible in writing of the nineteenth and earlier twentieth century—though not with greater candor or fidelity than literature of the Renaissance or the seventeenth or eighteenth centuries. Many persons are troubled not only by this less reticent character of current literature and films but also by the fact that many of the ablest and most serious writers of the day have located their most revealing delineations of human personality in sordid and violent circumstances.

And finally there are the nonfictional works discussing sex—many of them used in pastoral counseling: works on marital sexual relations, studies like those of Havelock Ellis, scientific inquiries like those of Dr. Kinsey, treatises on psychoanalysis, discussions of birth control, venereal disease, prostitution, and so on. These frequently arouse the most violent feelings of all.

. . . .

In the case of general literature and of factual and scientific work on sex, the question is not one of increasing volume but of increasing frankness, and this increase is evident, though it affects only a very small percentage of the total output of regularly produced films, magazines and books.

To what extent does the situation pose a moral crisis? Psychiatrists, psychologists, and experts on juvenile delinquency and the development of youth differ in some degree. Some see little or no ill consequence from exposure of normal youth even to criminal pornography; a very few even see possible indirect benefits from obscene materials that can divert into fantasy certain drives that might otherwise be expressed in antisocial acts. But most professional experts would agree that the exposure of children and youth to materials truly obscene is clearly undesirable. Few if any, however, see such materials as an element of major consequence in juvenile delinquency in comparison with such factors as broken homes, parental delinquency, slum surroundings, racial discrimination, school maladjustments or, for that matter, the turbulent sexual drives of adolescents, which exist quite independently of any external stimuli.

.   .   .   .

With respect to the moral standards of society generally, it seems clear that they are reflected in, rather than created by, the media of communication. Society had become quite tolerant of mild profanity in general conversation long before the first "Damn!" appeared on television, and the rather marked changes in sexual mores after World War I and again during and after World War II considerably antedated the franker treatment of sex in print. Whatever fundamental moral problem there may be probably exists within the standards of society itself; literature merely reflects the problem.

.   .   .   .

All of this is not to say that there is no cause for concern. The calculating commercial exploitation of sex in any manner is, to say the very least, distasteful and demeaning, and the existence of what the justice department has termed "hard-core" pornography is a continuing social problem of some proportions. But there seems to be little justification for the near-hysteria of some contemporary campaigns, and scant reason for apprehensiveness about ill consequences from reading general literature, no matter how frank.

What legal resources does society have for dealing with the problem? Some people claim that recent judicial decisions have weakened the ability of states and communities to control obscenity. It is true that for the first time in its history the Supreme Court has undertaken to clarify the confused state of the law regarding obscenity, and in so doing has doubtless curtailed the ungoverned power of police and local authorities to act in this field as they will. The principal effect of the court's recent decision has been to affirm that obscene films and publications do not enjoy the protection of the First Amendment and to define obscene films and publications as those that, in the absence of any redeeming social value, have as their dominant theme an appeal to the prurient interest of the normal reader, and that exceed the bounds of frankness tolerated in the community.

. . . .

Because the law is unwilling to extend its force so far as many would like to see it go, there is a strong temptation for the indignant to take the law into their own hands and use means of compulsion outside the courts to suppress what they personally believe [to be] objectionable. This is usually done in one of two ways. A public authority, usually acting under pressure from a citizens' committee, may draw up or adopt a list of books and magazines to which it objects and communicate the list to newsdealers and booksellers under such a color of authority that the publications are removed from sale. . . . The list may be locally compiled, or some national list, like that of the National Office of Decent Literature, may be used (though the N.O.D.L. has for some years vigorously objected to such a use of its list). For police or other governmental authorities to arrogate judicial powers to themselves in such a way is clearly illegal and has been regularly enjoined by the courts when appeal is made to them.

The other extra-legal form of compulsion employs private economic, rather than official, pressure and threatens with boycott the drugstore or newsstand that persists in selling publications included in a list to which a local committee objects.

. . . .

If compulsory measures are limited to those exercised by due process of law through the courts, and if the courts define obscenity more narrowly than many conscientious citizens would like, are such citizens left powerless to affect the character of reading materials available, especially those intended for youth? By no means. In all the great areas of human relations in which society seeks to improve the qualities of compassion, wisdom, and self-discipline with which we behave, it has found instruments more powerful than compulsion. We cannot through the courts force parents to be kind, nor can we force men to be wise by the pressure of committees. We have learned that education, example, the influence of public opinion are more powerful means to affect change.

. . . .

But one can go further. Most committees and organizations set up to deal with obscenity and related problems have "for decent literature" in their titles, but few do anything positive to bring good reading to the children and youth that most need it. By efforts to see that our children come to know the best of reading and by supporting better school libraries and public library service to children and youths we will do far more to make reading an uplifting and enriching experience than by any number of sporadic committee complaints about newsstands. . . .

For those whose concern for the troubled and rebellious youths we call delinquent is genuine, giving aid to remedial reading programs and making efforts through school programs, boys' clubs, youth centers, police athletic leagues and similar organizations to place in the hands of youngsters good books—books within their reading grasp, yet ones which can excite and enlarge their view of life and lead them upward and out of the narrow bounds they live in—can be infinitely more rewarding, if more difficult, then issuing manifestoes about "objectionable books." . . .

Finally, one must recognize that the cruelty and squalor and sexual anarchy portrayed in some publications unhappily reflect realities of life that young people will in any case encounter, and are encountering vicariously in newspapers daily, as they grow to manhood and womanhood. Life itself is often shocking, beset with temptation, surrounded with sordidness. The young people who meet these aspects of reality clearly and with integrity will be those who have been made aware of them and taught to confront them with understanding. . . .

President Kennedy and The Control of Pornography (1962)*

Q: Mr. President, a recent decision of the Supreme Court said that the Postmaster General does not have the authority to keep pornographic material out of the United States mails except in a limited way, and the most dreadful stuff is coming into our homes into the

---

*Excerpts from President Kennedy's news conference. John F. Kennedy, *Public Papers of the President of the U.S.: 1962* (U.S.: Government Printing Office, 1963), pp. 650–651. On October 19, 1962 President Kennedy vetoed H.R. 4670 designed to control "indecent publications" in the District of Columbia. The President cited *Marcus* v. *Search Warrant*, 367 U.S. 717 (1961) which brought into question the search and seizure aspects of the bill. He encouraged the new Congress to rewrite the bill.

hands of our children, brought by the United States mails. Now, have you or will you talk with the Attorney General and the Postmaster General as to how this can be remedied?

THE PRESIDENT: Well, the statutes on the distribution of pornographic literature are well, I am sure, known. There's always been a problem, of course, of what is pornography and what is not. And the courts have made judgments in regard to several well-known books recently which some people regard as pornographic and others regard as great literature. I would not make the judgment today.

I think it is a problem, not only in the mails but on the magazines, and it's a matter of concern for parents. I don't think that the Post Office can be expected to do anything but carry out the laws, nor can the Attorney General, and the laws, which are interpreted by the courts, are quite clear.

Clergymen, Obscenity and the Supreme Court (1964)*

Nine leading clergymen of Jewish, Protestant and Roman Catholic faiths attacked the Supreme Court for its apparent leniency in obscenity cases. The great fear was the Court's contribution to the breakdown of moral standards which, to the churchmen, were the backbone of the American system.

The Supreme Court of the United States virtually promulgated degeneracy as the standard way of American life. . . .

Under its debased standard, the Supreme Court approved a book which contains numerous passages unfit for printing either in a court decision or in a newspaper. . . .

In finding that the Constitution was intended as a guarantee for the dissemination of filth, and a device to deprive against vile and corrupt publications, the "under God" foundations of the United States were implied to be irrelevant. . . .

These decisions cannot be accepted quietly by the American people if this nation is to survive. Giving free rein to the vile depiction of violence, perversion, illicit sex and, in consequence, to their performance, is an unerring sign of progressive decay and decline. Further, it gives prophetic meaning to the Soviet intent to "bury" America.

---

*Reprinted with permission from *U.S. News and World Report*, September 21, 1964. p. 15.

A Book Named "John Cleland's Memoirs of a Woman of Pleasure" (1966)*

["*Fanny Hill*"] v. *Attorney General of Massachusetts*

In the following case the book *Fanny Hill* was put on trial and through the "redeeming social value" theory declared to be protected from an obscenity charge by the First Amendment. The opinion of the Court was delivered by Justice William Brennan.

This is an obscenity case in which *Memoirs of a Woman of Pleasure* (commonly known as *Fanny Hill*), written by John Cleland in about 1750, was adjudged obscene in a proceeding that put on trial the book itself, and not its publisher or distributor.

. . . .

The trial justice entered a final decree, which adjudged *Memoirs* obscene and declared that the book "is not entitled to the protection of the First and Fourteenth Amendments to the Constitution of the United States . . . The Massachusetts Supreme Judicial Court affirmed the decree. . . .

. . . .

We defined obscenity in *Roth* . . . Under this definition, as elaborated in subsequent cases, three elements must coalesce: it must be established that (a) the dominant theme of the material taken as a whole appeals to a prurient interest in sex; (b) the material is patently offensive because it affronts contemporary community standards relating to the description or representation of sexual matters; and (c) the material is utterly without redeeming social value.

. . . .

The Supreme Judicial Court erred in holding that a book need not be "unqualifiedly worthless before it can be deemed obscene." A book cannot be proscribed unless it is found to be utterly without redeeming social value. This is so even though the book is found to possess the requisite prurient appeal and to be patently offensive. Each of the three federal constitutional criteria is to be applied independently; the social value of the book can neither be weighed against nor canceled by its prurient appeal or patent offensiveness. Hence, even on the view of the court below that *Memoirs* possessed only a modicum of social

---

*383 U.S. 413.

value, its judgment must be reversed as being founded on an erroneous interpretation of a federal constitutional standard. . . .

In this proceeding . . . the courts were asked to judge the obscenity of *Memoirs* in the abstract, and the declaration of obscenity was neither aided nor limited by a specific set of circumstances of production, sale, and publicity. All possible uses of the book must therefore be considered, and the mere risk that the book might be exploited by panderers because it so pervasively treats sexual matters cannot alter the fact—given the view of the Massachusetts court attributing to *Memoirs* a modicum of literary and historical value—that the book will have redeeming social importance in the hands of those who publish or distribute it on the basis of that value.

Justice William O. Douglas concurred in a separate opinion.

I base my vote to reverse on my view that the First Amendment does not permit the censorship of expression not brigaded with illegal action. But even applying the prevailing view of the *Roth* test, reversal is compelled by this record which makes clear that *Fanny Hill* is not "obscene." The prosecution made virtually no effort to prove that this book is "utterly without redeeming social importance." The defense, on the other hand, introduced considerable and impressive testimony to the effect that this was a work of literary, historical, and social importance.

. . . .

Every time an obscenity case is to be argued here, my office is flooded with letters and postal cards urging me to protect the community or the Nation by striking down the publication. The messages are often identical even down to commas and semicolons. The inference is irresistible that they were all copied from a school or church blackboard. Dozens of postal cards often are mailed from the same precinct. The drives are incessant and the pressures are great. Happily we do not bow to them. I mention them only to emphasize the lack of popular understanding of our constitutional system. Publications and utterances were made immune from majoritarian control by the First Amendment, applicable to the States by reason of the Fourteenth. No exceptions were made, not even for obscenity.

. . . .

Whatever may be the reach of the power to regulate conduct, I stand by my view in *Roth* v. *United States*, . . . , that the First Amendment leaves no power in government over expression of ideas.

. . . .

Justice Tom Clark dissented in the following opinion.

It is with regret that I write this dissenting opinion. However, the public should know of the continuous flow of pornographic material reaching this Court and the increasing problem States have in controlling it. *Memoirs of a Woman of Pleasure*, the book involved here, is typical. I have "stomached" past cases for almost 10 years without much outcry. Though I am not known to be a purist—or a shrinking violet—this book is too much even for me.

.   .   .   .

Justice John Harlan also dissented in a separate opinion.

.   .   .   .

My premise is that in the area of obscenity the Constitution does not bind the States and the Federal Government in precisely the same fashion. . . .

Federal suppression of allegedly obscene matter should, in my view, be constitutionally limited to that often described as "hardcore pornography." . . . To me it is plain, for instance, that "Fanny Hill" does not fall within this class and could not be barred from the federal mails. . . .

State obscenity laws present problems of quite a different order. The varying conditions across the country, the range of views on the need and reasons for curbing obscenity, and the traditions of local self-government in matters of public welfare all favor a far more flexible attitude in defining the bounds for the States. From my standpoint, the Fourteenth Amendment requires of a State only that it apply criteria rationally related to the accepted notion of obscenity and that it reach results not wholly out of step with current American standards.

.   .   .   .

Justice Byron White added a third dissenting opinion.

.   .   .   .

If "social importance" is to be used as the prevailing opinion uses it today, obscene material, however far beyond customary limits of candor, is immune if it has any literary style, if it contains any historical references or language characteristic of a bygone day, or even if it is printed or bound in an interesting way. Well written, especially effective obscenity is protected; the poorly written is vulnerable. And why shouldn't the fact that some people buy and read such material prove its "social value"?

. . . .

In my view, "social importance" is not an independent test of obscenity but is relevant only to determining the predominant prurient interest of the material, a determination which the court or the jury will make based on the material itself and all the evidence in the case, expert or otherwise.

. . . .

Ginzburg et al. v. U.S. (1966)*

Although the materials themselves may not be obscene within the Court's definition, advertising which appeals primarily to prurient interests may be used to indicate the intent of the seller. It is not obvious that *Ginzburg* represents a step forward in the definition of obscenity law. The opinion of the Court was written by Justice William Brennan.

In the cases in which this Court has decided obscenity questions since *Roth*, it has regarded the materials as sufficient in themselves for the determination of the question. In the present case, however, the prosecution charged the offense in the context of the circumstances of production, sale, and publicity and assumed that, standing alone, the publications themselves might not be obscene. We agree that the question of obscenity may include consideration of the setting in which the publications were presented as an aid to determining the question of obscenity, and assume without deciding that the prosecution could not have succeeded otherwise. . . . we view the publications against a background of commercial exploitation of erotica solely for the sake of their prurient appeal.

. . . .

Besides testimony as to the merit of the material, there was abundant evidence to show that each of the accused publications was originated or sold as stock in trade of the sordid business of pandering—

---

*383 U.S. 463.

"the business of purveying textual or graphic matter openly advertised to appeal to the erotic interest of their customers." . . .

The "leer of the sensualist" also permeates the advertising for the three publications.

. . . .

We perceive no threat to First Amendment guarantees in thus holding that in close cases evidence of pandering may be probative with respect to the nature of the material in question and thus satisfy the *Roth* test.

. . . .

Where an exploitation of interests in titillation by pornography is shown with respect to material lending itself to such exploitation through pervasive treatment or description of sexual matters, such evidence may support the determination that the material is obscene even though in other contexts the material would escape such condemnation.

. . . .

Congress and Obscenity (1967)*

Congress has usually approached the problem of obscenity through controls administered by the Postmaster General and the Post Office Department. However, some aspects of such administration have been questioned by the courts. By establishing a special Commission, Congress hoped to provide guidance for future legislation to control pornography.

An Act to Establish a Commission on
Noxious and Obscene Matters and Materials

Section 1. The Congress finds that the traffic in obscenity and pornography is a matter of national concern. The Federal Government has a responsibility to investigate the gravity of this situation and to determine whether such materials are harmful to the public, and par-

---

*Congressional Record, September 20, 1967, pp. S13319–20. This Act became law in October, 1967 (Public Law 90-100).

ticularly to minors, and whether more effective methods should be devised to control the transmission of such materials. It is the purpose of this Act to establish an advisory commission whose purpose shall be, after a thorough study which shall include a study of the causal relationship of such materials to antisocial behavior, to recommend advisable, appropriate, effective, and constitutional means to deal effectively with such traffic in obscenity and pornography. . . .

. . . .

Section 5 (a) Investigation And Recommendations.—It shall be the duty of the Commission—

(1) with the aid of leading constitutional law authorities, to analyze the laws pertaining to the control of obscenity and pornography;

(2) to ascertain the methods employed in the distribution of obscene and pornographic materials and to explore the nature and volume of traffic in such materials;

(3) to study the effect of obscenity and pornography upon the public, and particularly minors, and its relationship to crime and other antisocial behavior; and

(4) to recommend such legislative, administrative, or other advisable and appropriate action as the Commission deems necessary to regulate effectively the flow of such traffic, without in any way interfering with constitutional rights.

(b) Report.—The Commission shall report to the President and the Congress its findings and recommendations as soon as practicable and in no event later than January 31, 1970. The Commission shall cease to exist the day following the submission of its final report.

. . . .

Obscenity and the Court: The Nomination of Associate Justice Abe Fortas to be Chief Justice (1968)*

The Senate is constitutionally obligated to give advice and consent to Presidential nominations to the Supreme Court. This obligation is one means by which Congress can control the high court. President

*Congressional Record, July 26, 1968, pp. S9439–9441.

Johnson's nomination, later withdrawn under pressure, of Associate Justice Abe Fortas to the Chief Justiceship presented critics of the Court an opportunity to express their concerns for court decisions in the area of obscenity.

MR. MILLER [Senator from Iowa]: Mr. President, before President Johnson announced his nominations to the Supreme Court, now pending before the Senate for confirmation, I announced that I would oppose confirmation of whoever might be nominated. The main reason was my belief that the people should have a chance to reflect their views on the direction our Federal Government should take through the election of a new President who, in turn, could reflect these views in appointments to the coequal branch of the Government—appointments which could last for 20 to 25 years, because they are lifetime appointments. Confirmation of these nominations would deprive the people of this chance. The rights of the people in this matter should override the right of the President to nominate and the right of the Senate to confirm.

. . . .

On the matter of judgment, the position of Justice Fortas on decisions of the Supreme Court with respect to two areas of national interest should concern every Member of the Senate; and they should have concerned the President before he submitted the nomination to the Senate.

The first is in the area of national security.

. . . .

The second area of national interest is the threat to the moral fiber of our people posed by the traffic in pornographic literature. On Monday of this week, the Senate Judiciary Committee received testimony from Mr. James J. Clancy, attorney, appearing in behalf of Citizens for Decent Literature, Inc. I happen to be on the national advisory board of this organization, and have been for several years. Its only purpose is to help preserve the moral standards of our States and communities by reducing and eliminating the traffic in pornographic literature. When decisions of the Supreme Court of the United States undermine this purpose and result in an increase in this traffic, it is understandable why the organization represented by Mr. Clancy would be concerned and why, further, it would oppose the confirmation of Justice Fortas when he participated in those decisions.

Mr. Clancy called attention to the fact that in May and June of 1967 the Court reversed 23 of 26 State and Federal convictions for violating laws on obscenity and that these upset the community standards of 13 States. Eight of these convictions were jury convictions. He also called attention to 26 more reversals in obscenity cases during the recent term of the Court ending last June. Justice Fortas voted with the 5-to-4 majority in all of these cases. All but three were decided without opinion, and in the three with an opinion there was only a brief majority opinion not written by Justice Fortas. In other words, we do not have his judicial philosophy on this subject; but we do have his judgment in the reversals of these cases, and the judgment is abhorrent to the maintenance of moral standards by our communities. It is judgment which encourages the permissiveness and criminal activity which are plaguing our society.

Testimony before the Senate Judiciary Committee also discloses that Justice Fortas voted to reverse a conviction in the case of Shackman against California, decided in June of 1967. In this case, three strip-tease films entitled "0-7," "0-12," and "D-15" were ruled hard-core pornography by Federal District Judge Hauk, a Los Angeles jury, and the California appellate system. All of these determinations were reversed, without opinion, by the Supreme Court in a 5-to-4 decision, with Justice Fortas casting the deciding vote.

.   .   .   .

The conclusion to be drawn from all of this is that those of my colleagues who speak of the need to do something about the flood of pornographic literature which is flowing through our mails and inundating our communities would be well advised to consider the role the Supreme Court has played in permitting this to happen. States like Georgia, Arkansas, Pennsylvania, New York, California, and Michigan, to name only a few of them, have had the moral standards of their communities practically destroyed by these Supreme Court decisions to which I have referred. Not long ago, a jury in the Federal district court sitting in my home town of Sioux City, Iowa, returned guilty verdicts on all counts of a 164-count indictment against a California publisher and distributor of nudist magazines and Lesbian-type paperbacks. The Circuit Court of Appeals for the Eighth Circuit, relying on these recent Supreme Court decisions, reversed the convictions. No State or community is immune to such an impact.

Now that these facts have been brought to public attention, I would hope that the President would withdraw the nominations.

Obscenity and the States (1969)*
New York State

The supreme court has jurisdiction to enjoin the sale or distribution of obscene prints and articles, as hereinafter specified:

1. The district attorney of any county, the chief executive officer of any city, town or village or the corporation counsel, or if there be none, the chief legal officer of any city, town or village, in which a person, firm or corporation publishes, sells or distributes or is about to sell or distribute or has in his possession with intent to sell or distribute or is about to acquire possession with intent to sell or distribute any book, magazine, pamphlet, comic book, story paper, writing, paper, picture, drawing, photograph, figure, image or any written or printed matter of an indecent character, which is obscene, lewd, lascivious, filthy, indecent or disgusting, or which contains an article or instrument of indecent or immoral use or purports to be for indecent or immoral use or purpose:... may maintain an action for an injunction against such person, firm or corporation....

2. The person, firm or corporation sought to be enjoined shall be entitled to a trial of the issues within one day after joinder of issue and a decision shall be rendered by the court within two days of the conclusion of the trial.

.   .   .   .

Pornography in the Privacy of One's Own Home (1969) †

Stanley v. Georgia

Does the state have the right to regulate the "enjoyment" of noxious forms of "art" within the privacy of one's own home? The Supreme Court in the following case rejected such control. The Court majority appeared to be accepting the permissive approach to artistic dissent. The opinion was written by Justice Thurgood Marshall.

An investigation of appellant's alleged bookmaking activities led to the issuance of a search warrant for appellant's home. Under au-

---

*Section 22a of the New York State Code of Criminal Procedure.
†89 S. Ct. 1243.

thority of this warrant, federal and state agents secured entrance. They found very little evidence of bookmaking activity, but while looking through a desk drawer in an upstairs bedroom, one of the federal agents, accompanied by a state officer, found three reels of eight-millimeter film. . . .

The state officer concluded that they were obscene and seized them. . . .

[Appellant] was later indicted for "knowingly having possession of obscene matter" in violation of Georgia law. . . .

Appellant argues here, and argued below, that the Georgia obscenity statute, insofar as it punishes mere private possession of obscene matter, violates the First Amendment, as made applicable to the States by the Fourteenth Amendment. For reasons set forth below, we agree that the mere private possession of obscene matter cannot constitutionally be made a crime.

. . . .

[Appellant] is asserting the right to read or observe what he pleases—the right to satisfy his intellectual and emotional needs in the privacy of his own home. He is asserting the right to be free from state inquiry into the contents of his library. Georgia contends that appellant does not have these rights, that there are certain types of materials that the individual may not read or even possess. Georgia justifies this assertion by arguing that the films in the present case are obscene. But we think that mere categorization of these films as "obscene" is insufficient justification for such a drastic invasion of personal liberties guaranteed by the First and Fourteenth Amendments. Whatever may be the justifications for other statutes regulating obscenity, we do not think they reach into the privacy of one's own home. If the First Amendment means anything, it means that a State has no business telling a man, sitting alone in his own house, what books he may read or what films he may watch. Our whole constitutional heritage rebels at the thought of giving government the power to control men's minds.

And yet, in the face of these traditional notions of individual liberty, Georgia asserts the right to protect the individual's mind from the effects of obscenity. We are not certain that this argument amounts to anything more than the assertion that the State has the right to control the moral content of a person's thoughts. To some, this may be a noble purpose, but it is wholly inconsistent with the philosophy of the First Amendment.

. . . .

We hold that the First and Fourteenth Amendments prohibit making mere private possession of obscene material a crime. *Roth* and the cases following that decision are not impaired by today's holding. As we have said, the States retain broad power to regulate obscenity; that power simply does not extend to mere possession by the individual in the privacy of his own home. . . .

"The Ultimate Answer Lies ... With ... The People" (1969)*

Richard M. Nixon

President Nixon, in a special message to Congress, outlined his administration's approach to the control of pornography.

American homes are being bombarded with the largest volume of sex-oriented mail in history. Most of it is unsolicited, unwanted, and deeply offensive to those who receive it. Since 1964, the number of complaints to the Post Office about this salacious mail has almost doubled.

One hundred and forty thousand letters of protest came in during the last nine months alone, and the volume is increasing. . . .

The problem has no simple solution. Many publications dealing with sex—in a way that is offensive to many people—are protected under the broad umbrella of the First Amendment prohibition against any law "abridging the freedom of speech, or of the press."

However, there are constitutional means available to assist parents seeking to protect their children from the flood of sex-oriented materials moving through the mails. The courts have not left society defenseless against the smut peddler; they have not ruled out reasonable Government action.

Cognizant of the constitutional strictures, aware of recent Supreme Court decisions, this Administration has carefully studied the legal terrain of this problem.

---

*President Nixon's Message to Congress. *New York Times* (May 3, 1969), p. 14.

We believe we have discovered some untried and hopeful approaches . . . I have asked the Attorney General and the Postmaster General to submit to Congress three new legislative proposals.

The first would prohibit outright the sending of offensive sex materials to any child or teen-ager under 18.

The second would prohibit the sending of advertising designed to appeal to a prurient interest in sex. It would apply regardless of the age of the recipient.

The third measure complements the second by providing added protection from the kind of smut advertising now being mailed, unsolicited, into so many homes.

Many states have moved ahead of the Federal Government in drawing distinctions between materials considered obscene for adults and materials considered obscene for children. . . .

The United States Supreme Court has recognized, in repeated decisions, the unique status of minors and has upheld the New York statute. Building on judicial precedent, we hope to provide a new measure of Federal protection for the young.

I ask Congress to make it a Federal crime to use the mails or other facilities of commerce to deliver to anyone under 18 years of age material dealing with a sexual subject in a manner unsuitable for young people.

.   .   .   .

The Federal Government would become a full partner with parents and states in protecting children from much of the interstate commerce in pornography. . . .

Many complaints about salacious literature coming through the mails focus on advertisements. Many of these ads are designed by the advertiser to appeal exclusively to a prurient interest. This is clearly a form of pandering.

I ask the Congress to make it a Federal crime to use the mails, or other facilities of commerce, for the commercial exploitation of a prurient interest in sex through advertising.

This measure focuses on the intent of the dealer in sex-oriented materials and his methods of marketing his materials. Through the legislation we hope to impose restrictions on dealers who flood the mails with grossly offensive advertisements intended to produce a market for their smut materials by stimulating the prurient interest of the recipient.

.   .   .   .

There are other erotic, sex-oriented advertisements that may be constitutionally protected but which are, nonetheless, offensive to the citizen who receives them in his home. No American should be forced to accept this kind of advertising through the mails.

In 1967 Congress passed a law to help deal with this kind of pandering. . . .

.   .   .   .

More than 170,000 persons have requested such orders. Many citizens however, are still unaware of this legislation, or do not know how to utilize its provisions. Accordingly, I have directed the Postmaster General to provide every Congressional office with pamphlets explaining how each citizen can use this law to protect his home from offensive advertising.

I urge Congress to assist our effort for the widest possible distribution of these pamphlets.

This pandering law was based on the principle that no citizen should be forced to receive advertisements for sex-oriented matter he finds offensive. I endorse that principle and believe its application should be broadened.

I therefore ask Congress to extend the existing law to enable a citizen to protect his home from any intrusions of sex-oriented advertising—regardless of whether or not a citizen has ever received such mailings.

.   .   .   .

As I have stated earlier, there is no simple solution to this problem. However, the measures I have proposed will go far toward protecting our youth from smut coming through the mails; they will place new restrictions upon the abuse of the postal services for pandering purposes; they will reinforce a man's right to privacy in his own home. These proposals, however, are not the whole answer.

The ultimate answer lies not with the Government but the people. What is required is a citizens' crusade against the obscene.

Supplementary Reading List

ABRAHAM, HENRY J., *Freedoms and the Courts* (New York: Oxford, 1967).

BARKER, LUCIUS J. and TWILEY W. BARKER, JR., *Freedoms, Courts, Politics* (Englewood Cliffs, N.J.: Prentice-Hall, 1965).

BECKER, THEODORE L., *The Impact of Supreme Court Decisions* (New York: Oxford University Press, 1969).

BERMAN, DANIEL M., *It Is So Ordered* (New York: Norton, 1966).

BETH, LOREN P., *Politics, The Constitution and the Supreme Court* (New York: Harper and Row, 1962).

CHAMBLISS, W. J., *Crime and the Legal Process* (New York: McGraw-Hill, 1969).

COX, ARCHIBALD, *The Warren Court* (Cambridge: Harvard University Press, 1968).

DIXON, ROBERT G., *Democratic Representation* (New York: Oxford University Press, 1968).

HART, H. L. A., *Law, Liberty and Morality* (New York: Random House, 1966).

JOHNSON, RICHARD M., *The Dynamics of Compliance* (Evanston: Northwestern University Press, 1967).

KRISLOV, SAMUEL, *The Supreme Court in the Political Process* (New York: The Macmillan Company, 1965).

LEE, CALVIN B. T., *One Man, One Vote* (New York: Scribners, 1967).

LEWIS, ANTHONY, *Gideon's Trumpet* (New York: Random House, 1964).

McCLELLAN, GRANT S. (ed.), *Censorship in the U.S.* (New York: H. W. Wilson, 1967).

McGRATH, JOHN J., *Church and State in American Law* (Milwaukee: Bruce Publishing Co., 1962).

MURPHY, WALTER F., *Congress and the Court* (Chicago: University of Chicago Press, 1962).

MURPHY, WALTER F. and C. HERMAN PRITCHETT, *Courts, Judges and Politics* (New York: Random House, 1961).

PRITCHETT, C. HERMAN, and ALAN J. WESTIN (eds.), *The Third Branch of Government* (New York: Harcourt, Brace and World, 1963).

PRITCHETT, C. HERMAN, *The American Constitutional System* (New York: McGraw-Hill, 1963).

REMBAR, CHARLES, *The End of Obscenity* (New York: Random House, 1968).

ROCHE, JOHN P., *Courts and Rights* (New York: Random House, 1961).

SCHUBERT, GLENDON, *Judicial Policy Making* (Chicago: Scott, Foresman, 1965).

——, *Reapportionment* (New York: Scribners, 1965).

TRESOLINI, ROCCO J., *Justice and the Supreme Court* (New York: J. B. Lippincott, 1963).

——, *These Liberties* (New York: J. B. Lippincott, 1968).

VOSE, *Caucasians Only* (Berkeley: University of California.

ZIEGLER, *Desegregation and the Supreme Court* (Boston:

DATE DUE

DEC 7 '71

DEMCO 38-297